W9-BLI-005

CAROLINE WREY'S
✳ *Complete* ✳
CURTAIN MAKING
COURSE

CAROLINE WREY'S
✳ *Complete* ✳
CURTAIN MAKING
COURSE

THE OVERLOOK PRESS
WOODSTOCK · NEW YORK

I would like to dedicate this book to my mother, Mary Clare Horn,
who taught me how to sew from a very young age.

First published in the United States in 1997 by
The Overlook Press, Peter Mayer Publishers, Inc.
Lewis Hollow Road,
Woodstock, New York 12498

Copyright © 1997 by Collins & Brown Limited

First published in Great Britain in 1997 by Collins & Brown Limited

Text copyright © 1997 by Caroline Wrey

Illustrations copyright © 1997 by Collins & Brown Limited

Photographs copyright © 1997 by Collins & Brown Limited;
unless otherwise stated; see copyright owners page 128

All Rights Reserved. No part of this publication may be reproduced, or transmitted in any form or by any
means, electronic or mechanical, including photocopy, recording, or any information storage and retrieval system
now known or to be invented without permission in writing from the publisher, except by a reviewer who wishes
to quote brief passages in connection with a review written for inclusion in a magazine, newpaper or broadcast.

Library of Congress Cataloging-in-Publication Data

Wrey, Caroline.
Caroline Wrey's complete curtain making course/Caroline Wrey
p.   cm.
Includes bibliographical references and index.
1. Drapery   I. Title
TT390.W6897   1997   646.2'1--dc21   97-7941

Printed and bound in France
ISBN 0-87951-803-09
2 4 6 8 9 7 5 3 1

Editor: Emma Callery
Designer: Janet James
Photography: Lucinda Symons

Contents

Introduction

For so many reasons, curtains are such an integral part of everyday life. Living with curtains which are both beautiful and perfect for the overall design of the room can only lead to a deeply happy mind and spirit due to the pleasure they inevitably bring not only to oneself (the creator), but also to the family in the house and all those special visitors. The joy is that the pleasure is gently reinforced on a daily basis since you are frequently drawing the curtains or at least looking at the outside world.

The window is one of the most important features of a room so it is essential to curtain it beautifully. After all, the curtains frame the view as well as softening the hard lines of the window. A good pair of well-made, high-quality curtains should have a life-span of at least 20 years. This life-span can easily be extended if you frequently use a roller blind (window shade) or have shutters to protect the fabric from the ultraviolet rays of the sun. It is also worth re-lining the curtains from time to time and only cleaning them very rarely; it is preferable to vacuum them instead. However reputable the cleaning company, I feel they never quite look the same again in terms of their glaze (if they are made of chintz) and the perfect length you had originally achieved may alter slightly. In my grandmother's house, the curtains still looked great after 45 years of hanging. They would have been cleaned occasionally and it is only fair to say that she did not live in a city and she used shutters.

You curtain a window for so many reasons apart from merely an excuse to be decorative. You need them for warmth but they have to be interlined to make a difference to the temperature of your room at night. Always interline – it is such a small percentage of work, in terms of the overall project. Yet the presence of that pure, thick cotton – within the curtains – makes all the difference in the world to both the professional look, let alone to the warmth in the room and the preservation of the fabric. There is something very cosy about shutting out the black night in the evening by drawing a beautiful pair of curtains. Privacy is also a major factor to which any form of curtaining will contribute.

I believe curtain-making to be one of the most creative pastimes in addition to being very therapeutic. (This is the same with sewing small items and dress-making.) An enormous amount of time, money and effort obviously goes into your project so then to see them hanging there, as a successfully completed project, can only give you the greatest pleasure in the world. I also love cooking and regard it as equally creative, but there is a fundamental difference here: cooking can create quite a lot of mess, both during the process and when lunch or dinner is over. In addition, when the delicious lunch or dinner is finished, there is nothing to show for it but a mountain of washing-up and everyone is hungry again a few hours later. Curtains, on the other hand, are a permanent feature and, once successfully hung, require no further attention.

Designing your perfect window treatment is the most enormous fun. I have laid out guidelines in this book to help you make all those fundamental decisions to guarantee a successful outcome (*see pages 10-17*). Having made them, you can then pick out one of the exciting new projects and execute it to make your window at home look beautiful. The projects in this book are so very, very easy that I can guarantee that anyone can follow the instructions even if they only enjoy sewing a tiny bit but really want to make one. Just follow each step, which is so clearly depicted in each wonderful colour photograph, and you can't go wrong – and the result is bound to be gorgeous. Before you begin, though, it is vital that you set yourself up with the correct equipment (*see pages 106-107*) to help you execute the project with ease.

Setting the Style

Before you even pick up a needle there are many design decisions to be made. Planning is just the beginning, you also need to consider your fabric choice, how the curtains are to be hung and any decorative details.

Planning

Your window treatment should reflect that you have given serious consideration to what the room is going to be used for and by who. For example, a dramatic look is perfect for halls, landings and dining rooms. Bullion fringing, big tassels, fixed curtain-headings, curtain hems 'puddling' on the floor, and low tiebacks are all dramatic details. For an elegant look in the drawing room, say, you will need to conjure up great comfort, beauty and luxury. Get maximum drops in your pelmets, curves if you can, and beautiful fringing. If you are after something more tailored, French, goblet, box, dovetail, and quintet pleats would each contribute to a very organized and even masculine look to the finished treatment.

Kitchens and bathrooms need to be warm and inviting. This is essential to dissolve any clinical or high-tech atmosphere. Floor-length curtains, curves of some description and very pretty details all lend themselves to the success of rooms such as these. Bedrooms should be as pretty as you feel like making them. It is essential that your bedroom is ultimately very peaceful for deep relaxation for either you or your guests. Try not to make the window treatments in children's rooms too childish and ensure

ABOVE This Roman blind is a perfect solution for this window. There is no housing space for curtains and it is important to keep maximum heat in the room at night, so the radiator must be exposed while still being able to shut out the night.

that they lend themselves to the best use of space. Blinds, of some description, are brilliant here as they allow for use of that valuable space under the window.

Whatever you do to a window, it must blend in with all the other items in the room. Therefore, if you have a lot of antique furniture, the faded chintz look would work well. However, if you have contemporary furniture, a more modern approach to your soft-furnishing project would be in keeping.

RIGHT A very grand window treatment on a stairway is exactly what you want as an eye-catching feature. The swags and tails fill the entire wall and the tails are correctly half the overall drop of the window treatment and rest conveniently just on top of the dado rail.

View

Always remember that your curtain treatment can never be divorced from the view. So it is good to take a quick look at the view in terms of its colours and character. When in the country, the view may well involve plenty of glorious colours, or at least lots of beautiful greens, therefore it probably isn't essential that you cover your interiors with endless floral prints. Also, if you do end up with a lot of green in your fabric, check it is the right green: bottle-green yew hedges in your garden would not be very well offset by lime green in your curtains. Equally, if you are in the city, it is lovely to have fabrics that are evocative of the country. For example, the ultimate faded chintz look is wonderful.

Ceiling height

When designing the perfect drop for a pelmet in any particular room there is one basic rule: the pelmet should be approximately one-sixth of the overall drop of the entire window treatment. The colour of the fabric and the amount of natural light in the room will also effect the ultimate drop. For example, a 50 cm (20 in) drop in a pelmet would look good in front of a 3 m (10 ft) drop of curtains. It is essential to avoid deep curves on pelmets when your ceiling drop is under 2.3 m (7 ft 6 in) as it would look disastrous. The great thing is that there are masses of ways to make a window treatment look very elegant or deeply outstanding by putting a huge emphasis on the headings and the trimmings, much of which this book is all about.

Equally, when wanting to gain as much height as possible, it is best to place your pelmet board as high as possible – even screw it into the ceiling. You then gain more space for the drop of your pelmet and cover that dead area of wall between the architrave and the cornice with lovely fabric. You also, very successfully, raise the overall height of the room.

But, of course, there are two further very important considerations to bear in mind before you can make your window treatment – fabric and the decorative trimmings. Fabrics are considered overleaf, and the trimmings on pages 14-15. For ideas on rails, poles and holdbacks, see pages 16-17.

ABOVE *A minimalist treatment here achieves an excellent harmony in the room since a lot of the furnishings are modern and simple. The steel pole blends perfectly with the steel light hanging.*

RIGHT *This rather grand and splendid window treatment is perfect for this formal room. Because the room faces south, the deep swag at the top does not render it too dark. Puddling curtains on the floor always add to a very lavish look.*

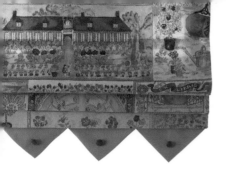

Fabrics

Fabric choice is obviously a matter of personal taste. We all have very strong likes and dislikes which is completely normal. But when attempting to choose the perfect fabric for a particular room, there are many points to bear in mind – most of which are worth deep consideration.

What does not help, in a sense, is that the choice of fabrics on the market is endless and can mesmerise you. Luckily, your well-defined personal taste and your budget (!) will produce firm boundaries within which you can work. First and foremost, whatever you choose must please your eye continuously. When you have the large sample hanging up – say, for at least a week – you must think that this is the one for you every time you walk into the room. You may be stunned by something at first glance but as you come to live with it, you may find you easily tire of it or else the fabric seriously begins to irritate your eye. It is also worth considering the feelings of the rest of the family who will have to live with it.

Remember that the natural light coming through the window will have a profound effect on the fabric you have chosen. In the northern hemisphere, south and west-facing rooms are very light, whereas north and east-facing rooms are much darker. The light is very strong from the west and the south so the fading factor is highly significant here. Therefore a roller blind (window shade) is a must. Yellow is one of the first colours to fade whereas those strong, rich, dark colours are more robust in terms of withstanding, to a certain degree, the intense ultraviolet rays. Also bear in mind the direction that

the room faces if you are trying to psychologically warm up a room. If the room faces north or east, stick to warm colours such as reds, pinks, beiges, yellows, rusts, terracottas, flames, and tomatoes, but if your room is south or west-facing, you do not have these concerns and can confidently use any colour with huge success.

Chintzes always look fresh and beautiful and have a terrifically lively feel because of their glaze which reflects a certain degree of light. Floral chintzes are particularly fitting in the city since it is lovely to have things around you that are evocative of the country. Whereas in a country house, there is not such a compelling need to hang floral material everywhere since you have got all that through the window.

Heavy linens, brocades and velvets have a more masculine image together with a lavish warmth. Remember, however, that they are possibly not as suitable for north and east-facing windows due to the slight lack of natural light. I think that silks are not used enough and sometimes you may find that they are often cheaper than many chintzes or linens. Silk does require the thickest interlining you can buy and roller blinds are then essential since fading and rotting (especially on the leading edges of the curtain) can occur very soon with such a delicate fabric on those south or west windows.

There are some wonderful heavy cottons on the market which hang beautifully on any window. The other fun thing to do with a window is to use a very inexpensive plain cotton, like calico, and then dress it up enormously by using a very elaborate trimming.

Trimmings and Tiebacks

These are definitely the 'icing on the cake' as your trimming reinforces the design qualities of your window treatment. Do not economise here – you will only regret it.

It is all these glorious finishing details which lead to the success and beauty of the overall window treatment. Elegant details provide the impact that the curtains deserve. Before deciding to add such details though, weigh up carefully which type to apply and to what extent; it is quite easy to overdo window treatments which could be disastrous if aiming for an elegant look. While I am very keen on beautiful details, it is vital to keep a perfect balance within both the window treatment and the room as a whole.

When it comes to trimmings, the sky is the limit in terms of choice. There is the most wonderful variety available on the market; it merely depends on what is most suitable for your window treatment or what you are prepared to pay. I would always err on the side of extravagance when it comes to trimmings since you will adore the effect and it will always give you pleasure. An economy at this point could lead to years of regret which would be tragic after all the effort that goes into creating a window treatment – it is rare that you can add trimmings once the item has actually been finished.

Trimmings that you make yourself are also equally beautiful and, in this case, there is possibly an even deeper feeling of satisfaction since you have actually made it yourself by using up the wasted fabric from the pattern repeats (this appeals to my Scottish blood!). For example, a Maltese cross (*see pages 37-38*) may be the perfect detail for you to use on your pelmet or curtain when a certain statement needs to be made. These are such elegant objects and are so easy to make. Or you may find that a pair of tiebacks will finish off your window treatment in the perfect way. In some cases, your window treatment may only be able to exist successfully if tiebacks are in place (*see pages 116-117*). Tiebacks definitely allow more light to fall into the room. They also give the curtains the most beautiful shape since the curtains will then hang with a 'swag' as opposed to absolutely straight. However, not all window treatments merit tiebacks; you do not want them to look like an unnecessary extra.

Poles and Holdbacks

It is quite a big decision you have to make as to whether you want a pelmet for your window or whether a pole would be more suitable. If you are going to have a pelmet, then you must only buy a strong metal rail (the telescopic type is the most practical) with an in-built pulley-system on which to hang your curtains. It is most advisable not to make do with an inferior existing rail which may be both dirty and antiquated. You must never draw curtains by hand since it is both a strain on them to yank them at a certain point as well as being bad for them to have your fingers (however clean!) touching them (there is a certain degree of acidity in all skin that fabric doesn't like). A good pulley-system allows the curtains to travel across the window with one single, fluid movement and without being touched. I am also very keen that you put brass acorns onto your pulley strings instead of using the provided plastic tensioner which you screw into the skirting board (although you would have to use the latter if your window is very wide and not very tall).

On the other hand, a gorgeous decorative pole is what you want if you are not going to have a pelmet. It is really worth buying a very super pole so that you achieve the maximum effect for your window treatment. They are available in all manner of styles and sizes and onto which you can either slip rings or make your own tab heads (*see pages 53-55*). Made in wood, brass or wrought or cast iron, there will be something that will suit the style of window treatment you are making, whether it is casual country or something more sophisticated. Stunning finials are equally important as the finishing touch and you will be able to choose from a wide range to match the pole.

You can buy the most sensational holdbacks in any big curtain hardware department. They screw into the wall wherever you want your curtains held back (at about the same height as a tieback), and then you can arrange the curtains behind them.

Curtains

*Curtaining a window is no
mean affair and in this
chapter ideas are given for
seven glorious different styles.
Starting with the essential
curtain – the fully interlined,
pencil-pleated variety –
complete with a pelmet, there
are then detailed instructions
given for fixed-heads and
more informal ways to hang
curtains without pelmets.*

Inspiration

There are so many different styles to choose from when considering a pair of curtains for your window whose heading is not covered by some glorious pelmet or other. You can make a great feature of your curtain headings and the pole off which they are to hang. Remember that a straight pencil-pleated heading is not designed to be exposed, whereas all the other ones featured here are.

There are three fixed-headings featured in this chapter: Italian stringing (*pages 34-39*), the puff ball (*pages 44-47*), and the high stand-up (*pages 48-51*). The puff-ball heading is a wonderfully contemporary-looking heading since it reminds me of a scrunchy for your hair. A thick heading with lots of gathering, it has a strong personality. You can pull this heading across a pole quite easily, but it is also brilliant as a fixed-head. It is mostly a machine-made heading, so pretty quick to do. The high stand-up heading is evocative of a caterpillar tieback and is definitely a fixed-head affair. Therefore, this would be no good to you if you are needing a lot of light in your room nor if you want warmth from interlining since it better to leave any bulk out of this one. It is a good heading if you want to try to raise the ceiling height of the room since the actual stand-up tends to take your eyes upwards. Italian stringing is another fixed-head, and slightly more complicated than the stand-up since this one involves hand-stitched rings. There is a big light loss with this too.

To go for a more intricate-looking heading, with fine details, a smocked-head such as that seen on pages 40-43 would be an excellent choice. Do not be put off by its many rows of stitches; this heading really doesn't take that long to do and is one of the most satisfying of all the curtain techniques.

For total informality, tab-heads are a charming way to hang a curtain (*see pages 53-55*). If they are too high above the floor, they will become hard to draw, yet they draw easily if they are somewhere just above eye-level. It is best not to interline these ones, though, because the additional weight will pull at the tabs, making them look very uneven. When curtaining a window using some types of sheer fabric, warmth cannot be one of your priorities. Sheers are brilliant for the introduction of a translucent quality into the room as well as privacy and a degree of light filtering (*see pages 56-57*).

ABOVE *Deep smocking is the most beautiful solution for a fixed-head set of curtains. The detail is so charming and the Italian stringing provides a perfect temporary door between the bedroom and the bathroom.*

ABOVE *These tab-heads are a fun way to hang your curtains when you want a less formal look. The sun picks up the yellow in the most lovely way.*

ABOVE *The combination of this puffball heading, over and above the 8 cm (3 in) line of smocking,*
is wonderfully frivolous and absolutely stunning for this elegant drawing room.
The fringing serves the essential purpose of accentuating the impact of the arched pelmet.

ABOVE *If you want to conjure up luxury, elegance, comfort and splendour, this is one of the ways you could do it.*
Not only do the poles make a very powerful statement, but the ropes and tassels underline this. In addition, there are two layers
of curtains, and only the second layer is drawn, leaving the front pair as dress curtains, designed not to be drawn.

RIGHT *The beautiful convex shape to the top of this pair of windows gives enormous interest and elegance to the overall style. The Italian stringing creates a pretty waterfall effect at the leading edges, accentuated by their fan-edge trim in a strong, dark, navy blue.*

BELOW *The translucent effect of voile curtaining allows this bathroom maximum light – the perfect way to be greeted at the beginning of each day. The voile is also very practical as it provides permanent privacy but without losing light.*

ABOVE *The sun shining through this starred voile has the most stunning effect on the way the light falls into this room. The metal pole, with its ram-horned finials, is a perfect way to hang such informal curtains.*

ABOVE *This simple pole offsets these informal curtains with ease and is an excellent treatment to accompany this contemporary check. The high brass holdbacks not only give a pretty shape to the curtains, but allow much more light to fall into the room.*

RIGHT *A pair of curtains on such small windows would have looked extremely peculiar, so asymmetry is a good, practical solution. Although they permanently cover half the window, the fact that the fabric is pale means loss of light is minimal.*

Above *Slotting curtains straight onto a pole accompanied by a high stand-up is an excellent way of drawing up your eye. The ruched blind behind allows for both privacy and the dark night to be shut out in the evening while still exposing the radiator for that precious heat.*

Left *This is an extremely decorative way of dealing with silk as a window treatment. Tab-headed curtains as high as this are hard to draw but the fact that they are so pale means that they are perfect as a fixed-head treatment, without too much light loss.*

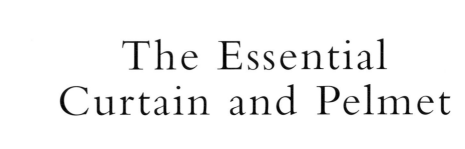

The Essential Curtain and Pelmet

NOTHING BEATS *a pair of beautifully made interlined curtains. The interlining is the essential ingredient that makes the overall look of the curtain so successful. Over the next four pages are instructions for making the perfect pair of interlined curtains, followed by the most simply made of pelmets on pages 32-33. The techniques used for this project are the core techniques of this book and in subsequent window treatments you will find that you are referred back to these pages. So my advice is to study these techniques especially carefully and you will realise just how easy it is to create the most beautifully made curtains and pelmet.*

Measuring

LENGTH: using a 2 m (2 yd) folding ruler, measure from the floor to the top of the window as described on page 108.

WIDTH: the length of the rail or pole and then add housing space on each side *(see curtain widths chart on page 108)*. Buy a pelmet board to fit this final sum *(see pelmet widths chart on page 109)*.

Cutting the fabrics

MAIN FABRIC LENGTH: to the finished drop length add 20 cm (7½ in): 12 cm (4½ in) for the hem and 8 cm (3 in) for the turn down at the top. They look brilliant like this but, personally, I then add 1 cm (½ in) because I like the curtains to just 'break' on the floor.

MAIN FABRIC WIDTH (PER CURTAIN): two-and-a-half-times the length of the pelmet board divided by 2. For the finished width of each curtain, always allow 10 cm (4 in) when pulling up the pencil-pleat tape, regardless of the size of the board. This extra will allow the curtain to cover with ease the added distance across the overlap arm and the returns into the wall.

INTERLINING: 10 cm (4 in) shorter than the main fabric, but the same width.

LINING: 10 cm (4 in) shorter and 10 cm (4 in) narrower than the main fabric.

MATERIALS

main fabric	*8 cm (3¼ in) wide*
lining	*pencil-pleat tape*
medium	*lead weights*
interlining	*brass hooks*

Attaching the Interlining

1 Join the drops of interlining by overlapping the fabric by 1.5 cm (⅝ in) and stitching with the biggest zigzag, selvedge to selvedge. You do not need to pin beyond the first 30 cm (12 in). Don't worry if this seam does not turn out completely straight and even. It is not a problem since the seam is incorporated invisibly within the gathered curtain.

2 Machine join the lining widths with a 1.5 cm (⅝ in) allowance. Turn up 3 cm (1¼ in), scrape along the fold with the metal ruler and then turn up again. Stitch and press.

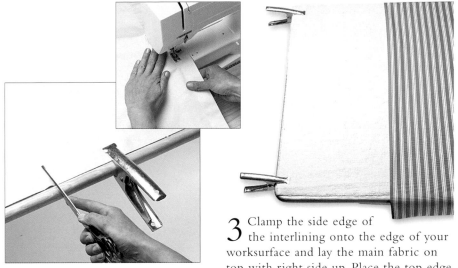

3 Clamp the side edge of the interlining onto the edge of your worksurface and lay the main fabric on top with right side up. Place the top edge of the material approximately 8 cm (3 in) above the interlining to allow for the heading. Fold back the side edge of the top material by 40 cm (16 in).

4 Make interlocking stitches *(see page 114)*, 10 cm (4 in) apart along the folded fabric, joining the main fabric to the interlining. Start or stop 20 cm (8 in) (a hand span) from the top edge of the interlining. Repeat these rows of interlining stitches approximately every 40 cm (16 in) across the curtain parallel with the selvedge. Very carefully turn over the fabric and interlining so that the main fabric is now flat on the table.

5 Turn back the interlining at the leading edge ready for more interlocking stitches. The easiest way to do this is to slip your little metal ruler between the interlining and the main fabric and turn the interlining back to the 5 cm (2 in) mark. Make more interlocking stitches on the interlining's fold, starting and stopping 20 cm (8 in) from the top and bottom of the curtain.

6 Turn the main fabric over the interlining at the side and make pyramid stitches *(see page 114)* down the seam, starting and stopping the stitches 20 cm (8 in) from the top and bottom as before. Repeat steps 5 and 6 on the other side of the curtain.

Making the Hem

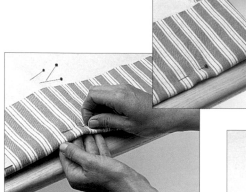

7 Turn up 12 cm (4½ in) along the bottom edge, pinning horizontally near the fold, and checking measurements as you work across the hem. At the corner, just turn up the 12 cm (4½ in) at this stage *(see detail)*. It is best and quickest to work with your small metal ruler.

8 Pull back the edge of the curtain material and trim away 3 cm (1¼ in) of the interlining.

9 Turn under 3 cm (1¼ in) of the raw edge of the main fabric over the interlining and pin the folded edge, moving the pins up from the bottom. Your turned-under hem will measure approximately 9 cm (3½ in) at this stage (anything between 8 and 10 cm [3¼ and 4 in] is fine). Leave the first and last 30 cm (12 in) un-pinned towards each corner.

Making Corners

10 Check the corner is a right angle against the table corner. Use the closed scissor blades to smooth any rucks from within the fold and then mark the corner with a long pin stuck in deeply.

11 Open out the hem and side seam until they are flat and trim the interlining, removing a rectangle as indicated. Cut around the outside edge of the pin which is marking the corner. It is imperative to remove this bulk to achieve a professional-looking corner.

12 Cut off a triangle of interlining from the corner marking pin to the bottom edge of the interlining (approximately a 45-degree angle).

13 Fold over the top fabric in a neat triangle and position a lead weight in the fold of the hem. Sew in place using strong buttonhole thread, doubled, and going over the edge of the weight. Make four stitches per hole.

14 Slip stitch *(see page 115)* the hem, working up the diagonal from the corner and along the top edge. Clamp at all times as it is an enormous help to both the success and speed of your sewing. You will achieve an easy, quick rhythm and acquire a natural tension to your hand-stitches.

Adding the Lining

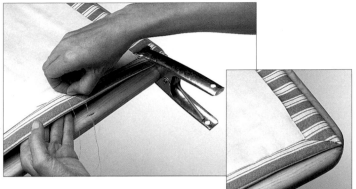

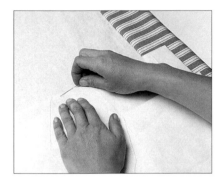

15 Align one of the side edges of the lining with the side of the curtain. At the bottom, leave 3 cm (1¼ in) of the main curtain showing beneath the lining. Clamp.

16 Fold under the edge of the lining to reveal 3 cm (1¼ in) of the main fabric at the side and slip stitch the lining to the curtain down the side edge. Start on the hem line, 3 cm (1¼ in) from the corner. The corner of the lining should align with the corner fold of the main fabric. It is imperative to use long slim needles at all times and especially here as it is the length of the needle that governs how far you can reach with each stitch. As a result, you can travel down the side of each curtain with great speed and then the project becomes a pleasure not a hindrance. Stitch to the bottom of the hem and 3 cm (1¼ in) along the bottom, but continue to stop stitches 20 cm (8 in) from the top.

17 Interlock the lining to the interlining every 40 cm (16 in), as before. Do not worry about positioning the stitches over the previous rows of interlocking. Make sure you make a few good anchor stitches at the bottom edge, since this is the only place the lining is attached at the hem. When all the interlocking stitches have been completed, repeat steps 15 and 16 on the other edge of the lining.

Making the Heading

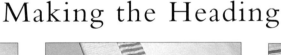

18 With a long ruler, measure from the hem up to the finished drop measurement of the curtain. Draw a pen line and then cut away both the interlining and the lining. Do not cut the main fabric. You will probably find there is very little interlining to cut away.

19 Fold over the main fabric and fold in the corners. Pin in place, with the pins running vertically up from the bottom.

20 Machine on the heading tape. Pin in place first, then fold under 1 cm (½ in) at the ends of the tape and pull out the three cords ready for pulling-up.

21 Pull-up the cords to the desired width and insert brass hooks into every fourth pocket. To make pulling-up easier you might like to use your clamps, as shown in step 2 on page 42.

Making the Pelmet

Measuring

LENGTH: one-sixth of the overall drop of the full window treatment.

WIDTH: the front of the pelmet board plus returns.

Cutting the fabrics

MAIN FABRIC LENGTH: twice the drop plus 3 cm (1¼ in) for seam allowances.

MAIN FABRIC WIDTH: three times the pelmet width measurement. Join as many widths together as necessary to fit this measurement.

MATERIALS

main fabric   *rope*

Velcro   *staple gun*

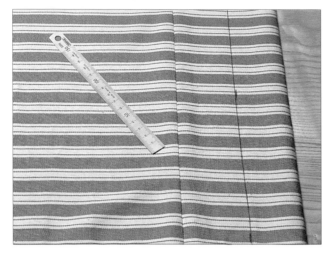

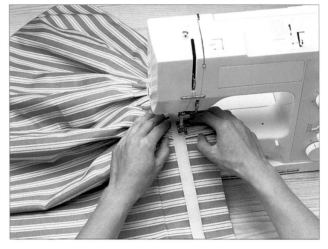

1 Fold the main fabric in half widthways with right sides facing and stitch together along the long seam taking a 1.5 cm (⅝ in) seam allowance. Turn right sides out and press so that the seam is quarter of the way down the back. As you press, ensure that the seam runs parallel to the top. Decide on the depth of your stand-up (here it is 5 cm [2 in]) and draw a line at this position along the wrong side of the pelmet. Turn in 2 cm (¾ in) at each end of the pelmet and slip stitch to close.

2 On the wrong side of the pelmet make 1.5 cm (⅝ in) pleats on the sewing machine, folding under the fabric, at the same time as attaching the Velcro. As you work you naturally get into a rhythm with your fingers and thumbs. To ensure a regular pleat (especially necessary on a striped fabric such as this), you might prefer to place pins at the top of the pelmet to represent the fold of each pleat. Frilling is easier since you don't have the size regulation to think about. Push the fabric with all your finger tips, lodging it under the machine foot as you sew. When you have finished sewing, you may want to press the heading, but I never do.

3 On the right side, hand-stitch the decorative finish in place on the pelmet. Here I have used a thick, soft rope. But you might choose a plait or caterpillar, perhaps with matching curtain tiebacks (*see pages 33, 116 and 117*). The pelmet is now ready to hang. Simply fix the other side of the Velcro level with the top of the pelmet board using a staple gun.

Detailing

This pelmet is quite extraordinarily quick to make once you get the hang of pleating or gathering straight onto Velcro. This is a wonderful technique to learn because the effect, in terms of a pelmet heading, is superb and very versatile, and you also have no need to hand-sew Velcro – not a thrilling task. A pleated top (as featured here) gives a sharper, more organized look, and a gathered one has a slightly softer look. The decorative detail hand-stitched across the top covers the machine stitches – so essential for a neat finish. Alternative finishes could be the plaited band or ruched band as illustrated below.

You can interline this pelmet, but it is much easier not to although if you were using silk it would be preferable. It is far easier to pleat-up without the interlining set in and you get a far sharper pleat to look at. All pelmets hang down so it is fun to produce one that 'stands up' as well. This is one of my favourite types of headings. The fabric we have chosen here is wonderfully simple with an understated look; it is very easy to live with.

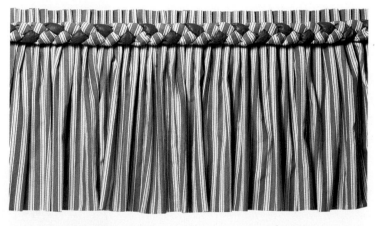

This plaited band is made as shown on page 116.

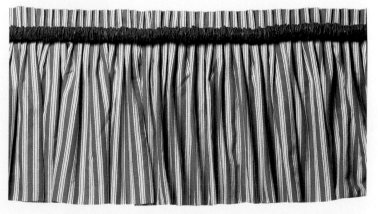

A ruched band: see the caterpillar instructions on page 117.

Italian Stringing and Maltese Cross

Because this window treatment has a fixed head, it is extremely eye-catching. It is particularly successful on windows that are not too wide (less than 1.30 m [1½ yd]) and those that face south or west because such a static heading blocks out a lot of light. This style is often used as dress curtains that have been deliberately designed never to be pulled, but they do, of course, pull up and release with extreme ease. This is a particularly good design of window treatment to use if you have a radiator under the window that cannot be moved. By adding a Roman blind and not releasing the Italian stringing in the evening, you achieve a stunning window treatment while still retaining the full heat in the room (and the night is shut out).

To give the window an even more interesting look, I have added a Maltese cross at the point where the curtains meet. This is a great addition to the window treatment as it is a beautiful focal point and brings the whole window treatment together in its centre. In addition, consider fixing the curtains on a board with a shallow curve on its top edge – no more than 15 cm (6 in) at its deepest point – screwed flat onto the wall exactly above the architrave. Again, the curtains hang off Velcro, hand-stitched as described overleaf, and fixed around the curved edge of the board. Velcro is wonderfully pliable, and easily curves around a gentle arch. The bottoms of the curtains will not run parallel to the floor. Instead, a lovely waterfall effect is created.

A further alternative way to hang these curtains is off a convex board that comes out into the room. The convex should be no more than 25 cm (10 in) at its deepest part in the centre, and the board must have no returns.

Measuring

As for Essential curtains on page 28.

Cutting the fabrics

As for Essential curtains on page 28.

MALTESE CROSS: cut two strips of main fabric measuring 26 x 47 cm (10 x 18½ in) (**strip A**) and 26 x 45 cm (10 x 17½ in) (**strip B**).

MATERIALS

main fabric
lining
interlining
15 cm (6 in) wide pencil pleat tape
lead weights
Velcro

plastic rings
thin nylon string
12 cm (4½ in) pelmet board
2 brass cleats
22 mm (1 in) self-covering metal button

Italian Stringing

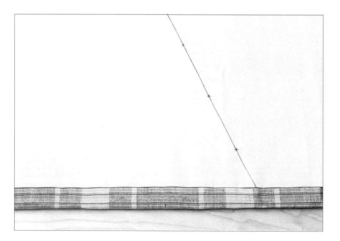

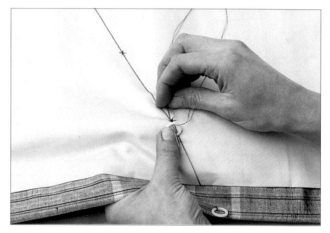

1 Make pencil-pleated curtains as described on pages 29-31, to step 20. Mark the leading edge where you would like the Italian stringing to begin (between ¼ and ⅓ of the way down) and mark the finishing point on the outside edge (usually 15 cm [6 in] higher). Join the points with a pen-drawn line across the back. Starting at the leading edge, mark every 10 cm (4 in) along the line.

2 Using doubled thread, sew on the plastic rings at each marked position making sure that you catch the main fabric with the thread. At the leading edge, anchor the ring very firmly using at least six stitches; thereafter three stitches per ring will be adequate. Cut off a sufficient length of the nylon string to go across the width of the curtain and tie it firmly to the ring at the leading edge. Then pass it through all the rest of the rings.

3 Pull-up the curtains to the required width. Stitch Velcro across the top of the pulled-up pencil-pleat tape aligning the top of the Velcro with the top of the tape. Hang on a pelmet board using the Velcro. If you are worried by the weight of your curtain and want to ensure a strong hold, bang in a few tacks between some of the pleats. When the curtains are hung, pull up the cord and attach it to the wall cleat fastened at an appropriate place behind the curtain.

Making a Maltese Cross

4 Taking the two strips of fabric, make two tubes by folding each strip in half lengthways with right sides facing and stitch together taking a 1.5 cm (⅝ in) seam allowance. Don't trim the seam, turn right sides out and press, swivelling the seam to centre back. Iron from the front. Then make two rings of fabric by slipping one end inside the other, pin in place and finally zigzag along the raw edge to finish.

Once the Maltese Cross is padded out and fixed in place it makes an extremely striking decorative feature.

5 Flatten each ring so that the join is in the centre back. Mark the finished pieces A and B to prevent confusion later on. A is the larger of the two rings.

6 Taking B, fold in half lengthways and mark the centre point on the front. Then unfold and pleat up both layers of fabric together to make four pleats.

7 Wrap an elastic band around the centre and puff up each end.

8 Hand stitch the pleats together using doubled thread. First stitch together the pleats along each side of the elastic band at the back and repeat at the front, stitching as near to the elastic band as possible. Cut off the elastic band.

9 Taking A, mark the centre front and back with a pen and then pleat the front and back separately, stitching the pleats on each side, as for B in step 8.

10 Slip B inside A with A running vertically. Pin together above and below the centre, both front and back. Stitch together the three layers with stabs (*see page 115*), working around the centre. Don't worry if your cross looks dreadful at this stage; it is quite normal!

11 Cover a 22 mm (³⁄₄ in) wide metal button with a suitable piece of fabric. Cut a circle of fabric that is 1 cm (½ in) wider in diameter than the self-covering button and then cover the button following the manufacturer's instructions. Stitch the button to the centre of the cross. Now really puff out and shape your Maltese cross with your fingers. To ensure the cross looks as full as possible, insert pieces of left-over fabric into the cross until it is severely stuffed.

*Curtains that are finished with Italian stringing are perfect for hanging in front of a radiator.
The stringing keeps the fabric well away from the heat.*

Smocked Heading

IF YOU WANT intricate details combined with prettiness, this is a glorious heading style. It has great interest and beauty which is essential when the tops of your curtains are to be exposed and you have chosen a special pole to offset your window treatment. Despite being such a very decorative window treatment, the overall effect is relatively understated – especially when loosely hung off a simple pole such as the one used here. Although the project here is for a bedroom, smocking looks good anywhere.

I love smocking – it is the most creative and therapeutic pastime. It is both easy and relaxing as long as you have the correct needle, and the results are instantaneous, which is doubly satisfying.

Measuring and cutting the fabrics

As for pencil-pleated curtains *(see page 28)*, but width per curtain should be half 2½ x length of the pole.
Make the curtains as for the pencil-pleated interlined curtains on pages 29–31 to step 19. For the heading tape, use 15 cm (8 in) wide pencil-pleat tape.

MATERIALS

main fabric

lining

interlining

lead weights

15 cm (8 in) wide pencil-pleat tape

embroidery skein

embroidery needles (long, fine darners with a large eye)

invisible marker pen (optional)

hooks

pole

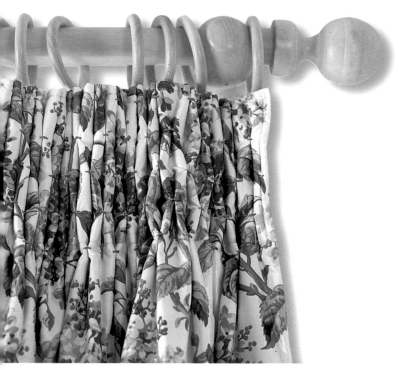

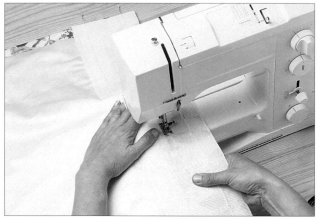

1 Stitch on the heading tape, stitching along the top, middle and bottom. It is important that the stitching is as straight as possible as it will be your guideline when making the smocking stitches. Also stitch vertically down each end to finish securely.

2 Pull up the heading to just over half the width of the pole and even out the front of the curtain fabric.

3 First smock the top row, working 1 cm (½ in) below the machine stitching. Working from left to right, pinch the first two pleats together. Pass the needle from back to front just to the left of this pleat – and then through the pleat right to left, as shown above. Finish the stitch by pushing the needle to the back in the same hole as the first stitch to the right of the pleat. Repeat with each subsequent pair of pleats, each time passing the needle through the curtain and round the back before stitching together the pleats.

4 Smock the bottom row in the same way, working
1 cm (½ in) below the bottom machine stitched line.
In this way you will get a slightly longer smocked
heading and you will also find it easier to get your
needle through fewer layers of fabric since you will be
avoiding the tape itself. Then measure carefully (you
could always use a vanishing marker pen) to find the
centre point between the top and bottom rows of
smocking and stitch along the centre in the same way.
The central machine line will be above this row of
stitching. Very soon your eye will easily 'tell' you where
the centre is, so you won't need to do any measuring
and the whole process will become quick and easy. You
have now smocked rows 1, 3 and 5.

5 Now smock the second row but working on
alternate pleats to those used for rows 1, 3 and 5.
Suddenly, your whole heading will come alive as it starts
to take its final shape. Smock the fourth row as for the
second, and you will then have your finished heading.

Variation: outlined smocked heading

*Here is a very smart
finishing touch to
a smocked heading –
and it is quick to do.
Using the same colour
of embroidery thread,
run a threaded needle
from stitch to stitch
working up and down
in a zigzag across
the smocked rows.
The smocking is then
successfully highlighted.*

6 The back of the curtain will
have long loops of embroidery
thread. Slot the hooks into the
heading tape spacing them
sufficiently far apart (approximately
10 cm [4 in]) to allow the curtain to
fold back when it is pulled open.

Puff-ball Heading

THE CURTAINS on this window treatment can never be opened completely. It is a very eye-catching heading and is especially enhanced by using a contrasting puff-ball section and also contrasting leading edges. The window treatment is equally successful if neither of these two sections are made from contrasting fabric. A further alternative would be to make an 8 cm (3 in) deep smocked heading (see pages 41-43) beneath the puffball (see page 21).

This is a perfect choice for a window if you do not want a pelmet yet like a flamboyant heading that has stature and presence. There is a huge variety of poles on the market so it is an easy task to pick the perfect one to enhance the colour scheme and style of your puff-ball curtains.

It is worth mentioning the light factor here; these curtains can never stack back too far because of their 'bouncy' heading so you will loose a certain amount of light with this style. You must also always add some sort of tieback or holdback with this style – not only to allow more light to fall into the room but also to create a beautiful shape to the curtains. Here I used caterpillar tiebacks (see detail overleaf), and instructions for making them are given on page 117. The best place to hang curtains of this style, therefore, would be on a south- or west-facing window and in not too dark a fabric.

It is always best to interline this type of curtain, but leave it out of the actual puff-ball section so it remains light and bouncy. An overall impression of this window treatment might be that it is complicated to make but you will see from the instructions overleaf just how easy it is to achieve.

Measuring

LENGTH: from the bottom of the pole to the floor.

WIDTH: The length of the pole.

Cutting the fabrics

MAIN FABRIC LENGTH: length of drop plus 12 cm (4½ in) for the hem and 1 cm (½ in) for the seam allowance at the top. If you would like the curtain to just break on the floor, add a further 1 cm (½ in) to these dimensions.

MAIN FABRIC WIDTH (PER CURTAIN): half 2½ x length of the pole.

LINING AND INTERLINING: the same as the main fabric.

CONTRAST STRIPS FOR THE LEADING EDGES: 13 cm (5 in) x the cutting length of the curtain.

CONTRAST STRIP FOR THE PUFF-BALL SECTION: 26 cm (10¼ in) x the cutting width of the main fabric. If you want an even bigger contrast than shown in the picture, you could increase the width of the strip to 30 cm (12 in).

MATERIALS

main fabric

lining

interlining

contrast fabric

lead weights

2 cm (¾ in) wide rufflet tape

brass hooks

substantial pole

tiebacks

tieback hooks

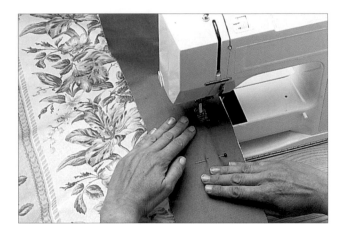

1 Pin and machine stitch the contrasting fabric for the leading edge to the leading edge side of the curtain fabric. Pin with right sides facing and the raw edges aligned and machine 4 cm (1½ in) in from raw edge. Use a strip of masking tape on the sewing machine plate to mark where 4 cm (1½ in) from the needle falls.

2 Press seam open and then fold the contrasting fabric over itself with the wrong sides together so that 4 cm (1½ in) remains at the front. Then make up the curtain as for the Essential Curtains on pages 29–31 up to and including step 17. With a long ruler, measure from the hem to the finished drop measurement of the curtain plus 1 cm (½ in) seam allowance. Draw a pen line and then cut away all three layers of fabric.

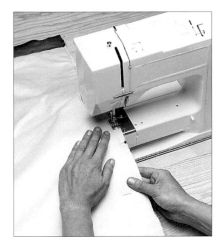

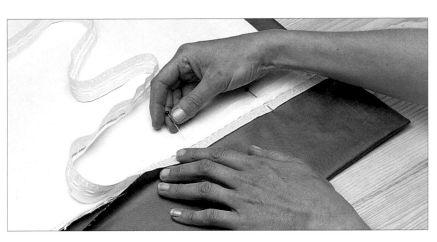

3 At the heading, pin and machine on the 26 cm (10¼ in) wide strip of contrast fabric. Pin with right sides facing and raw edges aligned and leave a 3 cm (1¼ in) allowance beyond the leading edge. Make a 1 cm (½ in) seam and press the seam towards the contrast fabric.

4 Fold the contrasting heading back on itself with wrong sides facing and let the raw edge lie 1 cm (½ in) below the joining seam. Pin on the narrow rufflet tape so that it covers the raw edge of the contrast and then machine stitch in place.

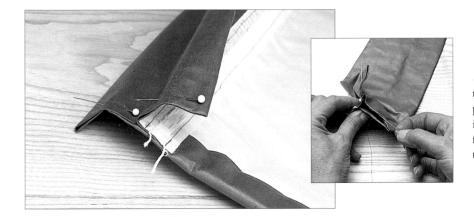

5 Push the contrast heading flat on itself, pin and then slip stitch the open ends. Remove the pins and press the rest of the heading so that it lies flat over the front of the main fabric. Pull up the tape and insert the hooks as in step 21 on page 31.

Detailing

These curtains have been held back with caterpillar tiebacks made from the contrasting fabric. Making instructions are given on page 117.

High Stand-up Heading

IT IS ALWAYS deeply tempting to use very 'adorable' fabrics when curtaining your child's room. However, think of all the time, money and effort channelled into them and then realise that that very sweet fabric might be outgrown within a few years. This is a shame since the average life of a curtain is at least 20 years. Therefore, why not choose something that you feel would be thoroughly acceptable to a teenager as well as a child? The fabric here, for example, is the perfect solution; it is stunning to look at, distinctive in its designs, intricate in its details, and appealing in its colours.

This type of heading is terribly easy to execute and is entirely machine-stitched. The high stand-up is a fixed-heading that is a glorious detail and balances so well with the fat ruche over the pole – and all offset by the attractive finials. It would also look wonderful with a choux rosette (see pages 118-119) attached at the centre. It is better not to interline this style of curtain, although, of course, it is perfectly possible (merely check that you trim the interlining right back at the lower machine line of the channel).

This is a very quick type of curtain to make, so it is a particularly satisfying project.

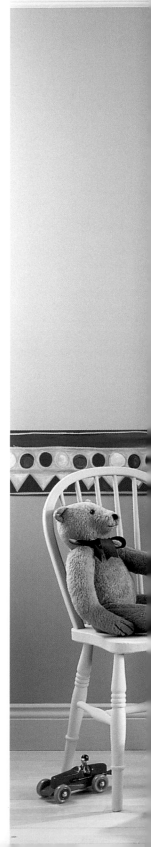

Measuring

LENGTH: fix the pole to the top of the window frame. Measure from the bottom of the pole to the floor. Also measure the circumference of the pole. This is exactly double the size of the channel to be machine-stitched. Add a 5 mm (¼ in) seam allowance, eg if the circumference of your pole is 8 cm (3 in), your channel should be 4.5 cm (1¾ in).

WIDTH: length of the pole.

MATERIALS

main fabric

lining

lead weights

pole with decorative finials

contrast fabric for ruched channel (optional)

tiebacks, holdbacks

Cutting the fabrics

MAIN FABRIC LENGTH: bottom of the pole to the floor plus the hem (12 cm [4½ in]) plus the channel size x 2, plus the stand-up (at least 7 cm [2¾ in] above the pole) x 2, plus 2 cm (¾ in) to turn under at back.

MAIN FABRIC WIDTH (PER CURTAIN): half 3 x length of the pole.

LINING LENGTH: bottom of the pole to the floor plus 3 cm (1¼ in) hem plus 1.5 cm (⅝ in) seam allowance at the top.

LINING WIDTH: as for main fabric.

1 Clamp the side of the fabric to the edge of the worksurface. Turn in a 5 cm (2 in) seam allowance on each side seam. Scrape with metal ruler and pin.

2 Turn up 12 cm (4½ in) at the hem, make right-angle corners and insert lead weights (*see step 13 on page 30*). Then turn under 3 cm (1¼ in) and pin in place. Slip stitch along the corners and hem. Line the curtain (*see steps 15-16 on page 31*) positioning the top of the lining 1.5 cm (⅝ in) above the line of the bottom of the pole. When slip stitching the side seams, stop 38 cm (15 in) below the raw edge at the top of the main fabric. There is no need to interlock this style since the head is fixed.

3 To make the 7 cm (2¾ in) high stand up and the pole channel, turn back 2 cm (¾ in) along the top and press. Fold back the rest of the fabric in half so that the turned back 2 cm (¾ in) rests on the top of the lining, pin and press again. The horizontal pin in the lining indicates where the slip stitching ended when attaching the lining.

4 Before machining the two parallel lines of stitches for the channel, open out the fabric flat and machine down the side hem from the top of the fabric to the lining, close to the edge, to prevent the pole from getting caught in the channel. Also cut off the corner of the folded over 2 cm (¾ in) for a neater finish. Fold over the fabric again and machine at the botttom fold, on top of the lining, and then again the width of the channel from the first line. Feed the pole through. Your ruching should be tight around it but not so tight that it is a struggle to feed on the curtain.

Detailing

*A plaited tieback is both smart and informal –
just right for a child's bedroom.
Making instructions are given on page 116.*

51

Tab-headed Curtains

THIS IS A VERY straightforward and easy treatment of a rather contemporary flavour. The curtains shown here are not interlined although there is no reason why you shouldn't as long as the curtains remain short otherwise the weight of a long drop would cause the buttons to pull. The tabs are shaped which makes them that much more interesting. Both ends of the tabs could have been stitched into the seam but it is fun to add the extra decorative quality of a button and select precisely the correct button for the tabs. An alternative is to stitch long, thin ties into the seam which you would then tie in bows over the pole. However, these can look rather untidy.

These tab-heads will always look organised and are guaranteed to behave well, yet they have a charmingly understated appearance. Presuming you do not use interlining, it may be advisable to add a second dimension to the window treatment in the form of a roller blind, for example. This will help to insulate the room and protect the fabric from the ultraviolet rays of the sun.

The curtains are featured here in a young girl's bedroom. However, these tab-heads also look brilliant in a kitchen, a bathroom, or in any room in a country cottage or beach house where life is relatively relaxed and the atmosphere can be enhanced by informal window treatments.

This is a very simple project that is easy to execute, which is particularly satisfying. Yet its simplicity requires careful and precise measuring and sewing to achieve the perfect result.

Measuring

LENGTH: from approximately 2 cm (¾ in) above the window down to 4 cm (1½ in) below the sill. The pole must sit well above the window so that at least 8 cm (3 in) of the tab can hang down below it on top of the curtain.

WIDTH: length of the pole.

Cutting the fabrics

MAIN FABRIC LENGTH: finished drop plus 12 cm (4½ in) for the hem and 2 cm (¾ in) for the top (seam allowance).

MAIN FABRIC WIDTH (PER CURTAIN): half 1½ or 2 x length of the pole plus 5 cm (2 in) at each side for turnings.

TAB STRIPS AND TOP FACING: see the step-by-step instructions overleaf.

LINING: 10 cm (4 in) shorter and narrower than the main fabric.

Making the Tabs

MATERIALS

main fabric
lining
lead weights
buttons
pole

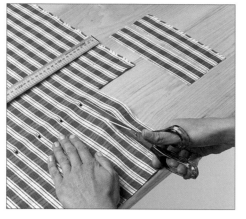

1 For each tab cut two pieces of fabric measuring 22 x 6 cm (8½ x 2½ in).

2 Cut a simple template out of card as shown above. The template must be the finished size of the intended tab. Place the template exactly on the centre of a stripe on the wrong side of the fabric and draw around it leaving at least a 1.5 cm (1 in) seam allowance around the sides and the point.

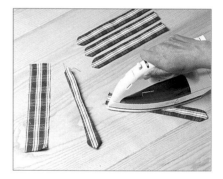

3 Machine stitch the tabs together in pairs with right sides facing and following the template marking, leaving the flat end open.

4 Trim around the tabs leaving 2 mm (¹⁄₁₆ in) excess.

5 Turn the tabs right sides out (help the corners by gently pushing each one with a pointed implement such as scissors) and press flat.

Making the Curtain

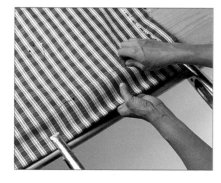

6 Clamp the main fabric to the edge of the worksurface wrong side up and turn back 5 cm (2 in) at each side seam and pin in place.

7 Turn up 12 cm (4½ in) at the hem, pin, make right-angled corners and insert a lead weight *(see step 13 on page 30)*. Slip stitch *(see page 115)* the hem.

8 Prepare the lining as in step 2 on page 29. Clamp on to the main fabric wrong sides together, turn the lining under by 3 cm (1¼ in) at each side, pin and slip stitch.

Making the Heading

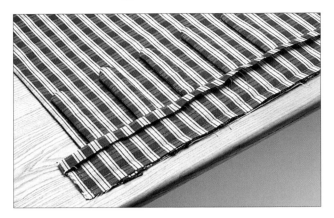

9 Pin the tabs in place at the top end of the curtain. Ensure the gaps between the tabs are equal (here the gap is 4.5 cm [1¾ in] and the tabs are positioned so that the white strip continues down the curtain). Also, the tabs lie 2 cm (¾ in) in from each curtain edge.

10 Cut the heading strip 8 cm (3 in) wide and 6 cm (2¼ in) longer than the stitched curtain width. Turn up 1.5 cm (⅝ in) along one long edge and press. Place the curtain heading on the main curtain with right sides facing, tabs in between, and raw edges aligned and 3 cm (1¼ in) excess at each end. Pin and tack, and then machine along the top edge taking a 1.5 cm (⅝ in) seam allowance.

11 Fold back the heading strip onto the curtain lining and fold in the excess heading at each end to neaten. Slip stitch the folded lower edge of the heading to the lining.

Variation: using gros-grain ribbons

Prepare the gros-grain ribbon by cutting 22 cm (8½ in) long strips. Then follow steps 6-11 above but inserting the ribbon folded in half lengthways between the heading and the top edge of the curtain. Sew a self-covering metal button below each ribbon to finish off the curtain.

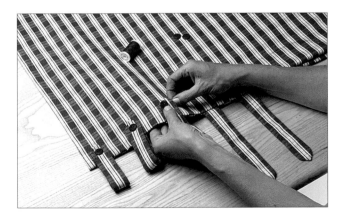

12 Bring the tabs over to the front of the curtain and sew the buttons in place to make the loops.

Rope-headed Sheers

THIS TYPE OF *window treatment has a gloriously translucent quality and must surely be the ultimate in terms of simplicity and understatement for any window. The effect of the voile is so beautiful, especially when the sun floods into the room. The print used here is very evocative of the sea. Of course, it would be good anywhere, but it would be especially suitable for a sunny holiday or beach house when formal curtains, smart chintzes and heavy interlining would be totally out of place.*

A large quantity (20 cm [8 in]) of voile draping onto the floor adds to the overall effect of a floaty, informal affair. The looping, natural-coloured rope on the top has a particularly nautical and beach-like character, and it is the perfect marriage for the voile. You could go further here and attach little shells to the rope (drill tiny little holes in each shell and stitch on). This is, of course, time consuming but so worthwhile for the stunning end result. Extravagant details in any window treatment are always so wholly worth doing for the pleasure they give for years to come. You only live to regret economies.

Measuring

LENGTH: from the top of the window architrave to the floor.

WIDTH: length of the pole.

Cutting the fabric

LENGTH: measured length plus 20 cm (8 in) for the extra voile on the floor plus 6 cm (2½ in) hem allowance plus 4 cm (1½ in) at the top for the turn down where the rope is to be sewn.

WIDTH (PER CURTAIN): half 1½ x length of the pole.

MATERIALS

voile

rope for heading

thin metal pole

1 At the hem, turn up 3 cm (1¼ in) and double it over. Pin and machine. Repeat for the heading, but folding over 2 cm (¾ in) each time. Let the selvedges hang freely. Carefully press the hem and heading.

2 Attach the rope with stab stitches *(see page 115)* using strong buttonhole thread and making rope loops every 9 cm (3½ in). To prevent the ends of the rope from unravelling, bind with thread and then dab with fabric glue.

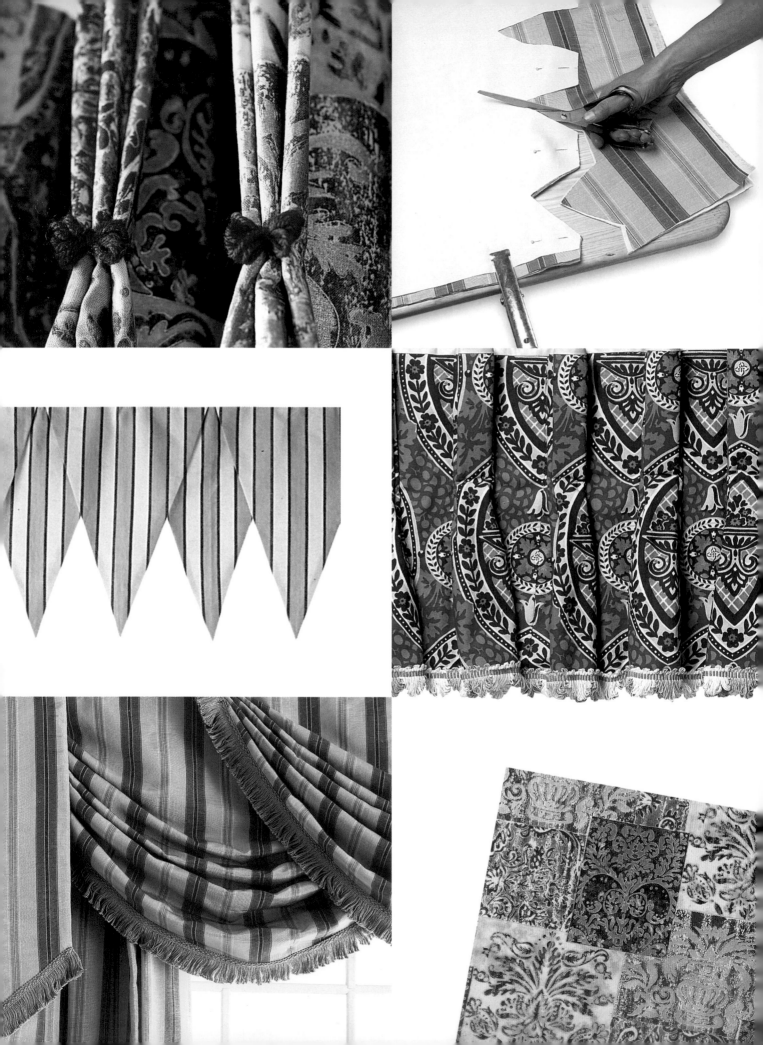

Pelmets

It is a big decision whether or not to have a pelmet (valance). Pelmets do look utterly wonderful in a room and they can only enhance the proportions of the window, let alone the overall decoration of the room. It is always tempting to make a pelmet of some description, but if your ceiling really is too low, look at the curtains on pages 34-57 where there are lots of ideas for windows without pelmets.

Inspiration

Once you have decided to have a pelmet, the big decision is – which type? Swags and tails (*see pages 80-87*) are, undoubtedly, the crown of all pelmets but you have got to have the ceiling height to be able to carry off such an elaborate pelmet otherwise the window would look swamped and the room totally overdone. They take a lot of fabric and are quite time-consuming to make since you have to design and cut a template first. But they are worth every minute of the time and effort invested in creating them.

You can have great fun deciding on the details that will suit your room and your own taste. I would always advise trimming the swags and tails with a fringe since they hugely emphasise the beauty of the pelmet with their graceful shape. You can self-line the tails with the main fabric or you can contrast face them, which may suit your overall look and add to the desired impact. One word of warning: I would never recommend a swag for a bay window as it can only fall plum if its top is absolutely straight, as opposed to being asked to curve around a 135-degree angle. A swag cannot curve properly and hang plum at the same time because it has no vertical gathering, only horizontal. There are countless glorious alternatives which look brilliant in bays – stick to them.

On the other end of the scale, a really fun pelmet, such as the harlequin one on pages 76-79 is brilliant for many types of windows whether yours is a tall, narrow one or a low, wide one. It is an extremely versatile pelmet since you can vary the proportions and the details considerably.

There are a huge number of straight-edged pelmets, all of which are gorgeous to look at. If you have a straight lower edge, it is well worth adding elegant details through trimmings and headings. French pleats are extremely elegant (*see pages 65-69*), while quintet or dovetail pleats are even more interesting (*see pages 70-71*). On the other hand, the self-pelmet at the top of a curtain is an extremely useful detail (*see pages 73-75*). There may be times that you want a pelmet or may want maximum light instead: here is the perfect compromise.

ABOVE *To add three-dimensional objects to a pelmet is so decorative and eye-catching. They also terrifically soften the formal look of a stiff pelmet.*

ABOVE *This self-pelmet is as informal as you can get with its tabs tied onto the pole and no interlining. The extra length in drop adds to the casual look.*

ABOVE *Deliciously thick, warm curtains in your bathroom make the room very cosy and inviting. Cutting out the cornice on the ceiling allows for even more height in the window treatment, which then enables you to cut an even greater drop in the pelmet.*

RIGHT *This very grand pelmet lends itself beautifully to this elegant and formal room. The curtains are just 'breaking' on the floor which gives the room an air of opulence. The fringing perfectly outlines the shape of the pelmet's lower edge.*

LEFT *The dog-toothing on this stiff pelmet is a perfect solution for this window treatment, set in a room full of decorative formality. The whole window treatment is tied together by the braiding outlining the pelmet's lower edge, its maximum height on the ceiling, its leading edges, its hem and also its tiebacks.*

BELOW LEFT *To dispense with fabric altogether and use wood instead for your pelmet is such a fun idea. Cutting decorative shapes with a jig-saw is not a hard task and then tying in the colour of your window frame to match the paint effect on the pelmet looks brilliant.*

BELOW *Dog-toothing with no stiffness behind also has an interesting effect, especially as you then get the light coming through the fabric.*

LEFT AND BELOW *Self-pelmets suspended off poles are the most brilliant way of treating a dining room in particular. This treatment means you can enjoy maximum light during the day yet have all the elegance of a pelmet at night. The fringing is essential as it accentuates the fact that there is a pelmet there.*

French-pleated Pelmet with Variations

THIS IS A HUGELY versatile pelmet, since you can put it anywhere and with many varying details and proportions to suit exactly the room you are designing it for. In a bedroom, for example, tailored pleats can be softened by details such as an inset fan-edge or small woollen fringe or a wool tuft stitched onto each pleat. Equally, you can make a far stronger statement (for a reception room, perhaps) by adding items such as contrast bullion fringing, knotted swagging rope, deep-coloured buttons and bound edges. On pages 70-71 there are two further stitching variations to make dovetail and quintet pleats.

This is a very easy pelmet to make indeed as it is entirely machine-made with a minute amount of hand-stitching (of the pleats and the Velcro) at the end. This is a very traditional pelmet which has an organised and tailored look. When using fusible buckram, always give the pelmet added support with a timber fascia to the front of the board (1 cm [½ in] deeper than the depth of the buckram) and also add timber vertical returns to the ends of the board to enhance the overall look of the returns of the pelmet (see the diagram, page 111).

Making the Pelmet

Measuring

LENGTH: one-sixth of the overall drop of the entire window treatment *(see page 11 for guidance)*.
WIDTH: the length of the board plus the two returns.

Cutting the fabrics

MAIN FABRIC LENGTH: the exact finished drop of the pelmet.
MAIN FABRIC WIDTH: 2½ x the length of the board plus the two returns, plus seam allowances at each end of 3 cm (1¼ in).
CONTRAST STRIP FOR THE TOP: width of the main fabric x 8 cm (3 in).
CONTRAST STRIP FOR THE HEM: width of the main fabric x 11 cm (4¼ in).
LINING LENGTH: 7 cm (2¾ in) less than the length of the main fabric.
LINING WIDTH: as main fabric.
INTERLINING: the same size as the main fabric.

Pleat length no more than one third of the overall drop of the pelmet.

MATERIALS

main fabric
lining
interlining
fusible buckram
metal buttons
contrast fabric
Velcro
17 cm (6½ in) deep pelmet board

1 Cut the widths of material, lining and interlining as outlined to the left. Join all the widths *(see page 113)*.

2 Make strips of contrast binding: that for the top should be 8 cm (3 in) deep; the bottom 11 cm (4¼ in). Join the widths, and sew the strips to the top and bottom of the main material, right sides together, with a 1.5 cm (⅝ in) seam. Here the bottom strip has been machined and pressed, and the top strip pinned, ready for machining.

3 Join the lining to the bottom contrast strip (which is already sewn to the main material), aligning the long edges and right sides. Allow the usual 1.5 cm (⅝ in) seam. At each end of this seam, finish the machine stitching about 7.5 cm (3 in) from each of the side edges. Press the seam from the right side of the material.

4 Turn the bottom contrast material and the lining over to the wrong side, so that there is 1.5 cm (⅝ in) of contrast showing on the right side. (This leaves the top edge of the lining below the top edge of the main material.) Press, clamping and measuring as you iron. Repeat with the narrower top contrast strip.

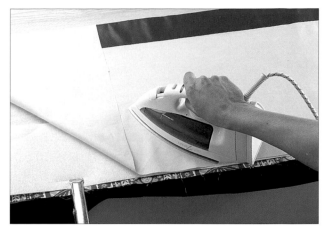

5 Turn the entire pelmet right over, so that the whole of the wrong side is facing upwards. Insert the joined widths of interlining between the main material and the lining, so that the piece fits exactly from the fold of the hem to the top raw edge of the lining. Then trim 3 cm (1¼ in) off both side edges of the interlining only.

6 Cut a piece of fusible buckram the same length as the pelmet. Insert it between the interlining and lining, matching its long edge to the raw edges of the materials. It is easiest to clamp the pelmet and buckram along the edge of the table. Iron the pelmet so that the buckram fuses to the lining and interlining.

7 On the raw edge of the top contrast material, fold over 1.5 cm (⅝ in) to the wrong side; press, and pin it in place. There is no need to sew it as the pleats, once stitched, will hold it in place.

8 Fold in the side edges of the main material about 3 cm (1¼ in) and press. Fold under both the lining and the contrast, so that there is a 2 cm (⅞ in) gap between the folded edge of the main material and the folded edge of the lining (concealing the interlining). Pin, and slip stitch (*see page 115*) everything in place.

9 There will not be any pleats on the pelmet-board returns (the two short sides next to the wall). Therefore, to start marking out the pleats, measure in from either side edge 17 cm (6½ in) and mark with a pin. Then measure in a further 5 cm (2 in) and insert another. Insert the pins vertically, with their heads protruding above the top edge.

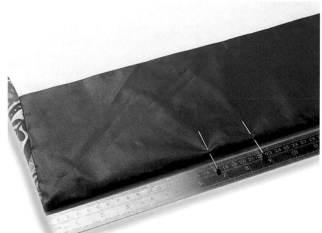

10 Calculate the number of pleats possible between the two inside pins. Each pleat will take up 10-15 cm (4-6 in) of fabric, with a gap between pleats in the region of 12-15 cm (5-6 in). Don't let the gap be too small or the pleats look crowded. It may help to draw a diagram to plan the number of pleats needed and the necessary measurements. Mark the side of each pleat and each gap with a vertical pin.

Making the Pleats

11 Fold each pleat wrong sides together, lining up the pins. Hold the pleat in place with a wooden peg or clothespin. Machine down the line indicated by the pins, starting about 1 cm (⅜ in) from the top and ending 15 cm (6 in) down from the top edge of the pelmet. When all the pleats have been stitched, check that the finished width of the pelmet fits around the pelmet board.

12 Lay the pelmet down on a flat surface, right side up. To form the three smaller pleats, hold the seam with one hand and the centre fold with the other. Push the centre fold downwards towards the table, so that the sides bulge out and the large single pleat forms into three smaller pleats. Pinch the three pleats together at the lower edge of the buckram and peg them at the top to secure.

13 Thread a needle with a matching double thread. Knot the end firmly, and insert the needle between two of the three pleats just below the buckram, so that the knot will be hidden eventually. Pull the needle out on one side of the pleats, and work three or four stitches backwards and forwards through all of the three pleats to secure them quite firmly, sewing below the buckram.

14 Take a self-covering button for each pleat, and cover with the contrast colour material. Sew a button to the base of each pleat, again using double, matching thread. Leave the pleats pegged with the clothes pegs (clothespins) for at least two to three days, to make the pleat tops look very sharp.

15 The soft side of the Velcro is now sewn to the back of the pelmet, with the top edges of the Velcro and the pelmet level. Pin it along the edge and hand sew it securely along the top, taking care that the pelmet does not 'shrink' or buckle as the Velcro is attached. Then sew around the Velcro and attach to the pelmet board.

Detailing

The short sides (returns) of the pelmet board do not carry any pleats: they start on the front of the board, 5 cm (2 in) along from each of the corners.

The pleats on this pelmet have not been stitched down at the top but at the bottom only, below the fusible buckram. For a tighter look, hand stitch the pleats at the top as well.

Making Dovetail Pleats

*The sand binding and fan edge here is obviously softer than
the navy trim and so more suitable when a quieter statement is required.
The scallop-shape to the fan edge is also a lovely soft touch – set-on
so that its pretty top is exposed, too. The flat face of the dovetail makes
it less pronounced than the very tailored-looking French or
quintet pleat. An easy way to start the fold of this pleat in step 1 is to
slip a flat ruler inside the main pleat and fold the first small pleat under it.*

1 Make the pelmet up to step 11
on page 68, making each pleat
17 cm (7 in) wide. Then flatten each
pleat and pinch one side with your
finger tips. Repeat on the other side.

2 Clamp the pleats at the top to
anchor them securely in place.
Stitch the pleat at the base, below
the buckram.

3 Using matching doubled thread,
stitch together the pinched
pleats at the top of each one, on
each side, through the chintz only.

70

Making Quintet Pleats

*This pelmet has a very strong presence and a more powerful message than the
French-pleated one. It is triple fullness which is necessary since each
pleat takes up 26 cm (10 in) of fabric. The navy bullion completely 'makes' the
pelmet. Not only does it tie-in with the navy binding but it accentuates
the gentle trumpet-shape formed below each quintet. This is a wonderfully attractive
alternative to the simpler French pleat.*

1 Make the pelmet up to step 11 on page 68, making each pleat 26 cm (10 in) wide. Then form the pleats by dividing each section into five. Using this measurement, fold the pleat into five.

2 Clamp the top of the pleats and stitch together at the base below the buckram using matching doubled thread. Finish the top of each pleat by stitching it to the top of the pelmet, but not the buckram.

Self-pelmet with Fringing

 THIS IS A BRILLIANT *window treatment if you want a pelmet at night (for elegance) yet want maximum light in the day as this type of design enables you to entirely draw the pelmet off the window. This is all set off by a very special pole and is very much suited to reception rooms, especially when they face north or east (the two darker directions in terms of light). A hall, in particular, would suit this treatment so well when you are keen to have maximum light in the day yet want a cosy and elegant look at night. Equally, in a dining room, this too can be the perfect solution so that the room is bright for lunchtime yet, in the evening with the curtains drawn, it is very sophisticated.*

This is a very easy window treatment to execute; it is very like the French pleated pelmet featured on pages 65-69, but even quicker to make since you only have to do one heading (as opposed to one for the curtains and one for the pelmet).

Measuring

LENGTH: one-sixth of the full curtain drop. Here it is 42 cm (16½ in).

WIDTH: same as the curtains.

Cutting the fabrics

MAIN FABRIC LENGTH: pelmet drop plus 8 cm (3 in) hem plus 18 cm (7¼ in) at the top (for the turn down, *see below*) – the width of the 15 cm (6 in) wide buckram plus 3 cm (1¼ in) seam allowance. To check the pattern match between pelmet and curtains, lay the pelmet fabric along the top of the curtain until the pattern matches. Allow at least 18 cm (7¼ in) turn down behind, and press.

MAIN FABRIC WIDTH (PER PELMET): the exact width of the flat finished curtain plus 5 cm (2 in) turning at each end.

LINING: same width but 25 cm (10 in) shorter than the length.

MATERIALS

main fabric	*15 cm (6 in) wide*
interlining	*fusible buckram*
lining	*wool for tufts*
bullion fringing	*pin hooks*

1 Make up the interlined curtains as for the Essential Curtains to step 19 *(see pages 29-31)*. On the pelmet, turn over 8 cm (3 in) at the hem and 18 cm (7¼ in) at the top and press firmly. Then machine-stitch the lining onto the hem with raw edges aligned and right sides facing and taking a 1.5 cm (⅝ in) seam allowance. Press the seam back against the main fabric. Mark the position of the fringe along the lower, pressed edge of the pelmet with a line of pins. Machine stitch in place.

2 Turn the pelmet wrong side up and position the fusible buckram along the top edge of the pelmet along the pressed line. Lay the lining over the top and then fold down the excess main fabric. Leave a fabric allowance of 5 cm (2 in) at each end of the buckram. Iron in place.

3 With the end of the pelmet firmly clamped to the edge of the table, trim the actual vertical fringing off the braid for 5 cm (2 in) beyond the end of the pelmet and stitch the excess to the back. Fold in 5 cm (2 in) of the fabric beneath the lining and pin and slip stitch the lining to the face fabric.

4 Place the pelmet on top of the curtain (whose top raw edges have been merely pinned) and fold back the top part of the main fabric (18 cm [7¼ in]) over the back of the top of the curtain. Mark out and stitch the pleats as described in the French pleat chapter (*see steps 9-13 on pages 67-68*) and stitch. To finish, stitch on hand-made tufts (*see page 122*). To hang the curtains, insert pin hooks into the back of the fabric behind each pleat so that the hooks are level with the top of the curtain.

Detailing

Finishing details can make all the difference to a pair of curtains. Here, small woollen tufts have been stitched to the bottom of each pleat. Making instructions for these tufts are given on page 122.

Harlequin Pelmet

A SENSATIONAL and original pelmet, this particular design is really fun to make and live with. On entering a room where a window is finished in this way, you could not fail to be struck by its pelmet. The triangles are only stitched together along the top as the essence of the look is that they are laid on top of each other and left to hang free. All that binds them together is their red contrast at the top, which is also an essential ingredient of the overall design. This particular pelmet is very light to hang on Velcro. Your greatest concern, then, is checking that you make the triangles totally identical in size.

A bay looks good when curtained as three individual windows instead of with one very large pair of curtains covering all three windows. There is no advantage in exposing the small section of wall that exists on either side of the central window. Instead, it is usually an improvement to have this section covered in lovely fabric.

The striped fabric used for this curtain was a great test when cutting out the triangles. You will see on the photograph opposite that it is always the darker stripe that reaches to the point. If using a similarly striped design, you will need to be aware of this to get the best possible result.

Measuring

DEPTH: approximately one-sixth of the finished curtain drop (however, remember that it is more important that your triangles work out to the size you want them to be in relation to the window and the fabric rather than sticking rigidly to the one-sixth rule).

WIDTH: the length of the board plus the two returns.

Cutting the fabrics

MAIN FABRIC AND LINING: see step 1 to the right.

CONTRAST FABRIC: enough strips approximately 7 cm (2¾ in) wide to join together to fit the width measurement.

MATERIALS

rough paper

main fabric

lining

contrast fabric

Velcro

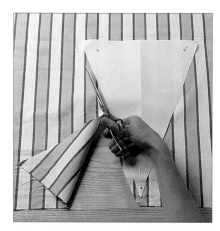

1 Cut out a triangular paper template so that the length is that of the pelmet drop. Pin the template onto the main fabric and, adding 1.5 cm (⅝ in) seam allowances around each side of the template, cut out enough triangles to overlap along the full length of the pelmet board and its returns. Cut an equal quantity of triangles from the lining fabric.

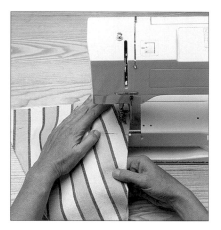

2 With right sides facing and raw edges aligned, machine together the face fabric and lining fabric triangles in pairs. Pin together first to ensure the fabrics don't slip and mark the end point most carefully with a pencilled cross. Leave the top edge open, trim the seams and turn right sides out. To ensure the point is sharp, use a pin on the right side of the fabric to carefully ease the last pieces of fabric through. Press.

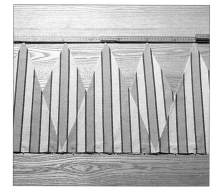

3 Position the triangles on your worksurface ensuring your best made ones are at the front. Align the points along the edge of a straightedge and pin the triangles together along the top.

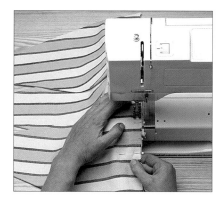

4 Machine stitch the triangles together, 1 cm (½ in) from the top and using a long stitch.

5 Machine stitch the contrast strip to the top of the harlequin pelmet with right sides facing and raw edges aligned. Take a 1.5 cm (⅝ in) seam allowance since this will then set the size of your finished binding. As you stitch, check that the triangles are lying flat.

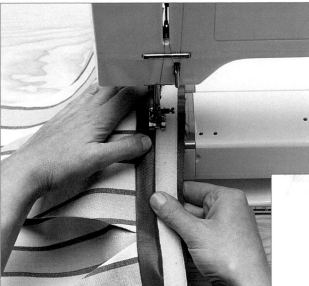

6 Press the contrast fabric to the back using a ruler as you work to ensure that the width showing at the front is consistent – 1.5 cm (⅝ in). Open the fabric out and machine the soft side of the Velcro to the contrast, aligning the top edge of the Velcro with the top crease. Machine stitch along each side of the Velcro and down its two ends.

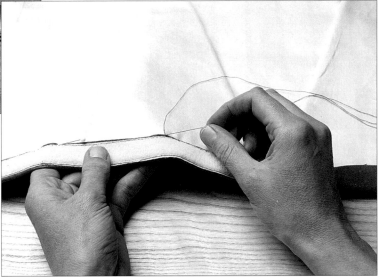

7 Pin the contrast fabric to the back of the pelmet with the excess fabric turned beneath. Slip stitch in place, ensuring the needle doesn't come through to the front. This is all too easily done as there is no interlining on this pelmet.

Detailing

The narrow strip of contrast fabric along the top of this pelmet sets off the stripes in the main fabric quite perfectly.

Swags and Tails

THIS PELMET MUST *be the ultimate in all window treatments and on correctly proportioned windows, swags and tails look quite wonderful. However, I would strongly advise you not to plan this type of window treatment for your room if it has a ceiling drop of less than 2.60 m (2¾ yd). The success of swags and tails definitely depends upon correct proportions throughout – the ceiling being the crucial factor.*

Again, the lowest part of the swag should be one-sixth of the overall drop of the window (see page 11); the lowest part of the tail should be half the overall drop. The shortest part of the tail looks good when it is approximately level with the bottom of the swag. The easiest way to hang these is to use both Velcro and webbing tape at various different points (see Hanging the Swags, overleaf). Use domette to interline the tails, as opposed to medium bump which is used in the swags. This enables the pleats to lie flatter so they look even neater and is strongly recommended.

You will see overleaf that I make my swag templates suspended on a false pelmet board rather than on the actual window pelmet board. Mine is made from a piece of 5 x 2.5 cm (2 x 1 in) batten with a screw-eye at each end so that the batten can be suspended from a pair of coat hooks on string. A false pelmet board is really the only way to execute this project since it allows you to experiment with the shape and size of a swag.

Once all three layers for the swag (main fabric, lining and interlining) are cut, they go together remarkably quickly, using a series of machine and hand stitches. We do suggest a zigzag stitch for the points of the swag (see step 10 on page 84), but you can successfully leave out this stage and still produce a beautiful swag.

Measuring

SWAG(S): the lowest point should be approximately one-sixth of the overall drop. Use string to ascertain the shape and width (*see step 1, opposite*).

TAILS LENGTH: let the longest point be half the overall drop and let the shortest point be approximately level with the lowest point of the swag once it has been pleated up.

TAILS WIDTH: see page 86.

Cutting the fabrics

SWAG: follow steps 1-5 opposite to make a template for the swags from lining fabric and then use it to cut the main fabric, lining and interlining as described in step 6, overleaf.

TAILS: follow step 1 on page 86 to make a scaled-down (¹⁄₁₀th of the real size) paper template and then use it to cut two pieces of main fabric and one of domette, as described in step 2 on page 86.

CHOOSING THE NUMBER OF SWAGS

window width	number of swags
under 1.20 m (1⅓ yd)	1
1.20-1.60 m (1⅓-1¾ yd)	2
1.60 m (1¾ yd) and beyond	3 or more

Hanging the Swags

There are two methods for fixing swags in place, both of which are covered in the instructions overleaf – webbing tape (see step 7) and Velcro (step 9). However, before making them you will need to be aware of the different methods of hanging swags as this determines which fixing method you will incorporate into yours.

ONE SWAG: centre this to the pelmet board and fix in place with Velcro.

TWO SWAGS: one swag overlaps the other. Make both to an identical width and the one that hangs behind, fix with Velcro. Make the other swag half with Velcro (the part that is fixed to the pelmet board) and the rest with webbing tape (the part that overlaps the other swag).

THREE SWAGS: make all of them to an identical width. For a window that is 1.80 m (2 yd) wide, for example, each one must measure 90 cm (36 in) across the top. Make two with Velcro and the third with webbing tape. To hang them, attach the Velcroed pair end to end and then add the webbed third swag centrally over the top.

FOUR SWAGS: hang perfectly symmetrically and with a continuous overlap, as for the two swags above. Swag 1 should be all Velcro; swags 2, 3 and 4 – first half webbing tape and second half Velcro.

MATERIALS

piping cord
lining
main fabric
interlining
fringing
domette
5 cm (2 in) wide webbing tape
Velcro

Making a Swag

1 Using your false pelmet board, clamp a length of piping cord to it to establish the size of the swag. Move the rope until the correct outline has been created, bearing in mind the measurements that you took for the width and the drop of the swag. Measure the distance from the top of the window to the lowest point of the draped piping cord. Unclamp the cord, tying a knot at each end where the cord joins the top of the false board so that you keep the cord to the exact length.

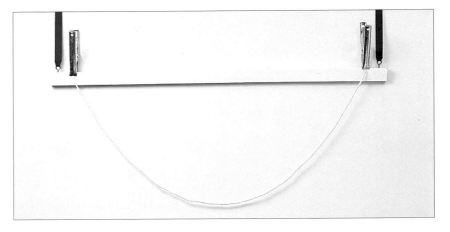

2 To make a template for the swag, fold a piece of lining in half vertically. Clamp onto the table. From the fold, measure along the top of the lining and mark A at half the width of the swag. Measure down the folded edge and mark B at approximately double the finished drop of the swag. Fold the piping cord in half and clamp on at B. Then make a gentle curve up towards the other side of the fabric and mark this point C (25-30 cm [10-12 in] higher than B). Join C to A with a long ruler, mark the line with a pencil and then cut. Draw along the cord from C to B and cut.

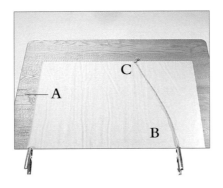

3 Still with the fabric folded in half, divide the length of A–C into five equal sections and mark the sections on the front of both sides.

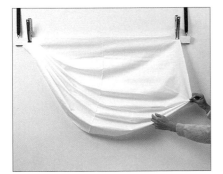

4 Open the fabric and clamp the top to the batten. Pleat up one side following the marks. Start from the bottom and work up, pinching a small amount of fabric at each pen mark and arranging the folds as you work. Leave a 5 mm (¼ in) step between each pleat as you work. Clamp the pleats in place and repeat on the other side following the draped folds to help guide you.

5 At each side, cut away excess fabric from the pleats. You will need to move the clamp in slightly towards the centre of the fabric (see the detail picture above) and press the creases firmly with the scissor blade before cutting. Repeat on the other side. Don't expect the finished cuts to be exactly symmetrical, this is almost impossible to achieve. Your template is now ready for your real swag. Only ever cut out a swag with the whole template lying flat on the main fabric.

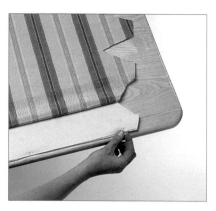

6 Unclamp the template and use it to cut out the real swag. First spread the interlining on the worksurface, and then the lining and main fabric with right sides together. Pin the template to the top and cut out all three fabrics together. Leave a 1.5 cm (⅝ in) seam allowance at the bottom and along the top edge. Remove the template.

7 If you are attaching webbing tape to the top of your pelmet *(see page 82)*, fold back the main fabric and pin the webbing tape to the lining and interlining along the top edge. Fold the main fabric back over the top.

8 For all swags (whether using webbing or Velcro), machine along the top and bottom of the swag taking 1.5 cm (⅝ in) seam allowances. Trim the excess interlining with scissors flat against the table to the machine line. Turn right sides out.

9 If you are attaching Velcro to the top of your pelmet *(see page 82)*, pin the soft part of it in place level with the top seam on the lining side and machine along each side and down the ends.

10 Press the top and bottom seams and pin the points in place. Machine zigzag stitch around each point as near to the edge of the fabric as possible.

11 Hand-stitch the fringe along the bottom of the swag. Pin first and then stitch leaving 4 cm (1½ in) excess at each end and the first and last 6 cm (2¼ in) unstitched.

12 Return to the batten and clamp the top edge of the swag in place, pulling it tight between the clamps. The fabric may bow a little at the top – don't worry. Starting from the bottom, pleat up one side as before and clamp in place. Then pleat up the other side, arranging the folds in the swag as you work, and clamp.

Detailing

A bullion fringe stitched along the bottom edge of your swags add to the luxury of this most exuberant of pelmets.

13 Keeping the clamps on the pleats, remove the swag from the batten and using matching doubled thread, stab stitch through the pleats to secure them. Make sure your stab stitches are underneath the first pleat so that they do not show. Don't worry about stitching the top pleat, this will be caught in the binding.

14 To finish the raw edges of the points, cut two pieces of lining 21 x 11.5 cm (8 x 4½ in) (you may find that the necessary size will vary). Press in 2 cm (¾ in) all the way round. Trim back the webbing and fold back 2 cm (¾ in), pinning in place. Then pin the lining binding over the pleats and hand stitch in place. It is possible to stitch both sides at the same time by stitching through the pleats. Repeat at the other end.

15 To finish the front, cut two pieces of binding from the main fabric, one for each top edge of the swag. Cut each one 11 cm (8 in) square (approximate size). Press in 1.5 cm (⅝ in) all around, pin in place at the front so that it goes over the back and hand stitch. Neaten the fringing by folding it to the back, over the binding, and hand stitch in place. The swag is now ready to be fixed to the pelmet board.

Making the Tails

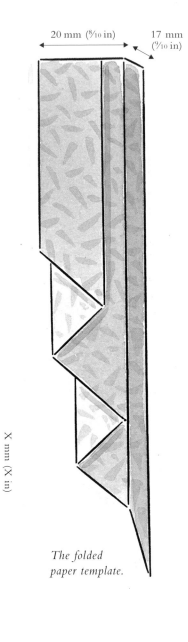

20 mm (⁸/₁₀ in)   17 mm (⁷/₁₀ in)

The folded paper template.

1 Before cutting any material, on rough paper make a scaled-down template, as illustrated below, making it ¹/₁₀ th of the real size of the tail. Use the measurements given below for the top edge (a tail looks good at 87 cm [35 in] wide before pleating) and add your own lengths for the inside and outside edges at X. Cut out the mini-template and fold A onto B and C onto D and fold back the return, checking that the measurements are correct. Open out again.

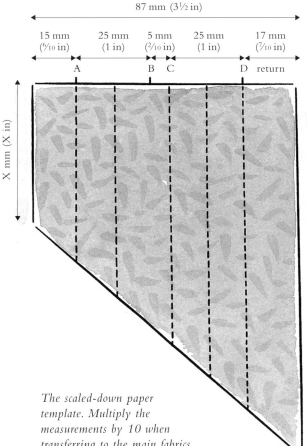

87 mm (3½ in)

| 15 mm (⁶/₁₀ in) | 25 mm (1 in) | 5 mm (²/₁₀ in) | 25 mm (1 in) | 17 mm (⁷/₁₀ in) |

A   B C   D return

X mm (X in)

X mm (X in)

Tails are always made in pairs – and these instructions are for the right tail. Reverse all the instructions for the left tail.

The scaled-down paper template. Multiply the measurements by 10 when transferring to the main fabrics.

2 Lay the domette on your worksurface followed by the two layers of the main fabric, laid out with right sides facing. There is no contrast lining for these tails as they are self-lined. Mark out the width (90 cm [36¼ in], including 1.5 cm [⅝ in] seam allowances) and drops of the inside and outside edges (ensure you are including 1.5 cm [⅝ in] seam allowances at top and bottom) on the top fabric as indicated on the scaled diagram using a pen and ruler, and cut out all three layers together. For the drop, see page 81.

3 Before machine-stitching, cut off the two lower corners of domette to give a neat finish once the tails are turned through. Machine stitch together all three layers with a 1.5 cm (⅝ in) seam allowance. Work down one side, starting 4 cm (1½ in) from the top, go across the bottom and up the other side, stopping 4 cm (1½ in) from the top. Trim the domette around all three sides. Press the seams and turn through. Press again.

4 Lay the tail on your worksurface with the wrong side face up. At the top, fold back the back piece of main fabric by 4 cm (1½ in). Mark the domette 4 cm (1½ in) from the top and cut off the excess. Fold in 4 cm (1½ in) seam allowances on both front and back fabrics at the top edge, neatening the corners as you reach them. Pin in place.

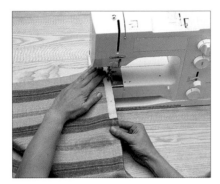

5 Pin on the soft side of Velcro on the tail return (17 cm [6¾ in]) leaving 2 mm (¹⁄₁₆ in) of the back fabric showing above the Velcro. Stitch along the top of the Velcro, down the end, along the bottom edge and back up to the start.

6 Clamping the top edge of the tail to your worksurface, slip stitch the top to close. Hand-stitch the fringe in place, as for the swag, applying it to the diagonal edge only. Leave 2 cm (¾ in) excess at each end, double the fringe under and stitch in place to neaten.

7 Transfer the pleat measurements from the scale drawing to the fabric, marking the positions of the folds with pins. Make the pleats by folding A onto B and C onto D, as on your scaled-down template (see opposite).

9 Sew on two 15 cm (6 in) lengths of webbing tape which will be used to fix the tail to the top of the pelmet board. On each piece of webbing, fold back one end by 2 cm (¾ in) and hand stitch it to the back of the tail. Position the first piece 1 cm (½ in) in from the short edge of the tail and 2 cm (¾ in) down from the top. Position the second piece over the first pleat. Hang the tail by hanging the Velcro around the pelmet board's return and attaching the webbing with a staple gun.

8 To fix the pleats, use matching doubled thread and overstitch across the pleats along the top edge.

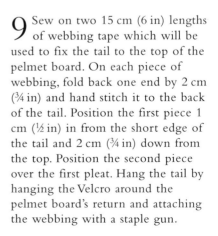

Blinds

Some windows benefit from a less ornate treatment, and others can only be covered with a blind as space is restricted. The Roman blind is a stylish and simple solution. It can be dressed up with ornate edges and stylish details should you want something a little more unusual.

Inspiration

A Roman blind is a highly practical yet very smart type of design for a window treatment. It does have a somewhat minimalist character, yet this can be exploited in many ways. So, you can keep the design deeply simple and functional (if that is what suits you and the particular room you are designing for), or you can seriously 'dress up' the blind with gorgeous details such as dog-toothing along the bottom edge (*see pages 94-99*) or contrast bindings (*see pages 100-103*).

Kitchens often lend themselves to Roman blinds. If you have units up to windowsills, floor-length curtains are obviously an impossibility. Equally, if you have built-in cupboards very close to your window recess or architrave, there is no housing space for a conventional type of curtain to pull back to. From a practical point of view, too, short, gathered curtains can be terribly in the way in terms of sinks and cookers. So, some sort of blind is the only alternative. If there is a little space below the sill, you can indulge in a decorative lower edge detail such as the dog-tooth style shown on page 94.

It is worth taking a great deal of trouble when producing a Roman blind since they are unforgiving creatures. This does not mean to say they are difficult to make; they are not. They merely require precision measuring and sewing. Unlike straightforward pencil-pleated, interlined curtains, where alteration on site to both length and width is simple, the Roman blind is unalterable once made.

It is always vital that the hanging and the finish is perfect on a blind: no nasty grey strings hanging down all over the place or visible Velcro on the board, or a lower edge that does not hang absolutely parallel with the windowsill or floor. I love to substitute as much string as possible with an attractive bell-pull cord. Buy a decent brass cleat for the wall or architrave to wrap the rope around. It is these finishing details that add to the overall success of the window treatment. You never want things to look tacky or cheap. Always strive for the most professional look – never mind if it is a tiny bit more effort, it is worth every minute.

ABOVE *This sheer has the most beautiful, delicate quality – accentuated by the tiny pear-shaped crystals suspended from each dog-tooth.*

BELOW *The minimalist quality of these Roman blinds is perfect in this simple kitchen, devoid of clutter and any other heavy window treatments.*

ABOVE *Shutters and attractive casements mean that conventional curtains would present a problem here. Therefore, blinds are the perfect solution. The subtle green blends beautifully with both the garden and the wooden floor. The gently curving lower edge softens what would otherwise have been a rigid look.*

RIGHT *Here the curtains are simple and unpelmetted, so the addition of a Roman blind with a dog-toothed lower edge adds a charmingly decorative quality to this dining room.*

BELOW *This soft roller blind has a charmingly original quality by being lined in a contrasting colour. When pulled up, a new dimension is revealed.*

ABOVE *Roller blinds made out of striped fabric look brilliant. This fits the recess so perfectly yet its regimented character is somewhat softened by its gently curving lower edge, with its blue outline to accentuate it.*

ABOVE *These roller blinds are extraordinarily decorative, to the extent that they not only have a dog-toothed pelmet above, but also long ties to hold them up (but don't expect your six-year-old daughter to manage to pull these up every morning!).*

RIGHT *To put a soft pelmet above a Roman blind can be the perfect happy medium between a fully curtained window and merely a blinded one. This works very well and allows for the total exposure of pretty ornaments on the window sill.*

Roman Blind with Dog-toothed Edging

PLAYING WITH a Roman blind's hem is always tempting since this adds an interesting shape to what would otherwise be merely a rectangle. The dog-toothing along this particular blind's lower edge is made very simply from squares of fabric folded along the diagonal and then in half again to make small and neat triangles (see steps 6-7 on page 98 for a detailed description of how to make them). They give a blind a whole new presence.

Correct details are vital for the ultimate success of any window treatment so always bear in mind the addition of eye-catching details since these can make them unique to you. Here, for example, small self-covered buttons have been stitched onto each dog-tooth. The fabric chosen to cover them is in a strong contrasting shade to the dog-tooth, but you might decide to use a similar shade or even the fabric from which the blind itself is made. Playing around with such details is always enormous fun.

You can make a blind like this very wide indeed (up to 2.5 m [8 ft]) with enormous success. It is imperative that the diameter of the doweling rods is then 1.5 cm ($^5/_8$ in) and that your vertical stringing is every 50 cm (20 in).

Measuring

Measure the required finished size of the blind exactly, both height and width. For this style of blind, remember to allow space for the dog-toothed edging.

Cutting the fabrics

MAIN FABRIC: exactly this size plus 5 cm (2 in) seam allowance on all four sides. Bear in mind pattern-matching as you plan your cutting lengths *(see page 113)*. Also, remember that with any blind, it is always essential that you have the whole width in the centre with equal parts of widths on either side. Perfect symmetry is vital.

LINING: the exact finished width of blind. To the finished blind length, however, add 5 cm (2 in) for each rod you intend to insert in the blind *(see step 3)* (you are going to machine-stitch channels in the lining for the rods) and a further 3 cm (1¼ in) top and bottom.

CONTRAST FABRIC: see the step-by-step instructions overleaf.

The rod pockets are usually between 18 and 22 cm (7 and 8½ in) apart. Estimate how many you will need for your blind (here, stopping at the point where the dog-toothing is attached) and then establish the exact positioning of each pocket. An ideal situation for rod positioning is as follows:

• 20 cm (8 in) between each rod
• 25 cm (10 in) between the highest rod and the top of the blind
• 10 cm (4 in) between the lowest rod and the finished hem.

You can vary these measurements a little, but try not to reduce the distances at the top and bottom.

Cutting the timber

LOWER EDGE BATTEN: 5 mm x 5 cm (¼ x 2 in) x the width of finished blind.

DOWELING RODS: 1 cm (½ in) in diameter (1.5 cm [⅝ in] if blind is over 1.8 m [6 ft] wide) (one per every 20 cm [8 in] of blind length) x width of finished blind less 6 cm (2¼ in).

MOUNTING BATTEN: 2 x 5 cm (¾ x 2 in) x the width of finished blind.

CHANNEL ALLOWANCES
(PER ROD)

size of doweling (diameter)	channel allowance
1 cm (½ in)	5 cm (2 in)
1.5 cm (⅝ in)	6 cm (2¼ in)

Preparing the Blind

MATERIALS

main fabric

lining

contrast fabric

stapler

doweling rods

mounting batten

Velcro

metal self-covering buttons

screw eyes

plastic rings

cord

decorative rope pull

brass wall cleat

bradawl

screw driver

1 Press a 5 cm (2 in) seam on each side of the main fabric, folding a right-angled corner at each point. Open out the fabric and fold in the corner on the diagonal to make a neat mitre. Do not do any stitching at this point. On the lining, turn in 3 cm (1¼ in) all the way around and make mitres as for the main fabric. Machine the hems and press.

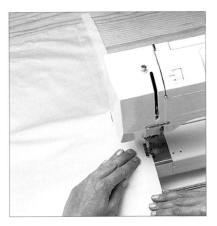

2 On the right side of the lining, pin and machine the soft Velcro (do not use the self-adhesive type). Leave a 3 cm (1¼ in) allowance at each end. To make slip stitching later on much easier, position the Velcro so that it is 2 mm (1/16 in) down from the top edge.

3 Starting from the bottom edge of the lining, mark out the rod channels so that they are the relevent distances apart (*see opposite*) and each rod channel is 5 cm (2 in) wide. It is very important that your measuring should be totally accurate and each channel must run parallel to the top and bottom seams. Measure precisely and mark the lines with pen. The pen lines will not show so do not worry about it. To make the first rod channel, fold the lining with wrong sides facing so that the bottom pair of drawn lines are on top of each other. Pin and machine stitch. Repeat with each subsequent pair of lines.

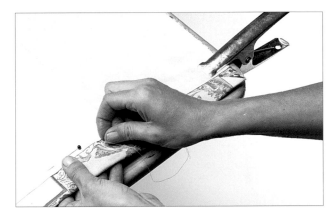

4 Clamp the main fabric face down on the table and place the lining on top with the wrong sides facing, leaving a 3 cm (1¼ in) gap between the sides of the fabric and the lining. Align the lining at the hem and top of the main fabric, pin in place, and then slip stitch up the sides starting at the bottom channel and leaving the channels free. Leave the bottom open.

5 Pin the lining channels through to the front of the main fabric. Machine in place, through the machine lines beneath each rod channel flap.

Making the Dog-toothing

6 Cut out 20 cm (8 in) squares for the dog toothing. Fold each square of fabric in half diagonally and then in half again and press neatly, making sure all the edges align. You do not ever need to sew these. The folding and ironing is enough to hold the triangle perfectly. Place the Roman blind, face down on the table and slip in the flat batten at the hem. Position the dog toothing triangles along the blind's lower edge (which is already folded), overlapping each triangle as much as you think is necessary, depending on the scale of your blind. Here they are overlapped by 5 cm (2 in). Once you are happy with the positioning, staple the triangles through onto the thin wooden batten, inside the hem. This is easier than pinning since it is hard to pin through so many layers of chintz and you also do not want to disturb your careful arrangement of triangles. Bring down the lining.

7 Slip stitch the lining in place (only stitching through one layer of chintz) and neaten the corners. Use a good sharp needle.

8 Insert a rod into each lining channel at the back of the blind and hand-stitch the end of the channels to keep the rods in place. Sew on plastic rings to the rod channels on the blind. Place them 12 cm (5 in) in from each side of the blind. Unless your blind is more than 1.35 m (4 ft 6 in) wide, you will only need two cords to pull it up.

9 Finally, stitch on a button in the centre front of each dog tooth as a smart decorative finish.

Preparing the Batten

10 Cut enough fabric to go around the batten with an overlap and allow 4 cm (1½ in) extra at each end to make a neat fold. Wrap the fabric around the batten and staple in place. Neaten the ends with diagonal folds and staple in place, too.

11 Position the hard Velcro along the top edge of the front of the batten. It doesn't matter if you use plain or adhesive Velcro, but either must be stapled in place for stability.

12 Use the bradawl to make holes in the bottom edge of the batten and then put in screw-eyes. The position of the eyes corresponds to the plastic rings which will hold the blind cord in place, plus an additional one at the end through which all the cords will be fed.

Hanging the Blind

13 Screw the batten flat onto the wall wherever it suits you. The ideal place is sitting above, and probably flush with, the architrave. Place the wall cleat on the architrave.

14 Following the diagram, right, feed the string that is furthest away from the wall cleat up from the lowest ring, making a firm knot at this point. When the string reaches the batten, feed it through the screw eye and turn 90 degrees to the right, channelling it through the other screw eyes on the batten. Repeat with each successive row of rings until the whole blind is strung up and then fasten in place.

15 Attach the decorative rope pull and use an S-hook beyond the last screw eye. Knot and sew the string to the top half of the S-hook. Attach the rope pull to the other half.

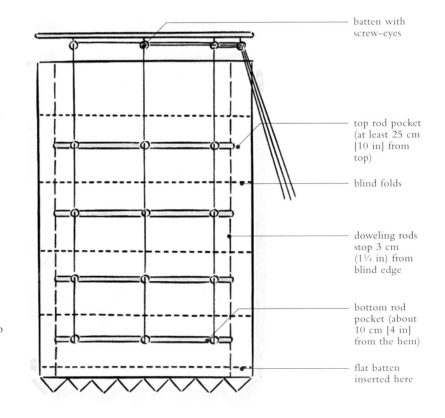

batten with screw-eyes

top rod pocket (at least 25 cm [10 in] from top)

blind folds

doweling rods stop 3 cm (1¼ in) from blind edge

bottom rod pocket (about 10 cm [4 in] from the hem)

flat batten inserted here

Roman Blind with Contrast Border

THIS IS AN EXTREMELY *smart and elegant way of finishing a window, especially if you want a very unfussy look with no gathers. There is a touch of minimalism here. Equally, if you are keen to have the architraves of your window exposed or you want to make maximum use of the wall space on either side of the windows (you might have small pictures you want to hang or furniture you want to place), a pair of Roman blinds like these are the perfect solution. Their strong red contrast is an excellent finishing touch for the style of this room, adding colour and flair to a simple situation. Introducing a positive solid colour like this helps lead the eye onto other objects in the room.*

As with the Roman blind featured on pages 95-99, these are not hard to make but they do require very careful measuring and precision sewing. The position of the red border in relation to the other stripes on the main fabric is very significant in terms of the overall success of the design of the window treatment. When planning how to cut the fabric, I found that it was imperative to have a space between the red border and the solid red stripe on the main fabric for a perfect balance.

Measuring

Measure the required finished size of blind exactly, height and width.

Cutting the fabrics

MAIN FABRIC: the required finished size of the blind.

LINING: as for the Roman blind on page 96.

CONTRAST FABRIC: for each side border cut strips that are 15 cm (6 in) wide and the same length as the blind plus 5 cm (2 in). For the bottom border, cut a strip 15 cm (6 in) deep and the same width as the blind plus 10 cm (4 in).

MATERIALS

main fabric	*screw eyes*
lining	*plastic rings*
contrast fabric	*cord*
stapler	*decorative rope pull*
doweling rods	*brass wall cleat*
mounting batten	*bradawl*
Velcro	*screw driver*

1 On each vertical side, pin the contrast to the main fabric, aligning the raw edges at the top and down the side and with right sides facing. The contrast strip should extend 5 cm (2 in) beyond the bottom edge of the blind. Stitch in place taking a 5 cm (2 in) seam allowance. If you are working on a striped fabric, as here, stitch with the stripes upwards so that you can accurately stitch along the pattern. Repeat down the second side and press the contrast open, then fold the contrast over the main fabric's raw edge and press. Open out flat once again.

2 Repeat for the bottom border, pinning the strip along the blind's lower edge with right sides facing and raw edges aligned. Machine stitch 5 cm (2 in) up from the bottom edge, but start and finish exactly where this strip meets the two vertical strips already stitched in place. Fold over the bottom border and press flat.

3 To make neatly mitred corners, fold back each corner of the bottom border at a 45-degree angle, and pin onto the edge border. Slip stitch (*see page 115*) to keep in place.

4 On the back of the blind, fold back the excess contrast fabric and pin in place. Make a mitre on each of the bottom back corners, as before, and slip stitch the mitres with lots of small stitches. Continue making up the Roman blind following steps 2-15 as on pages 97-99.

The contrast border on this Roman blind clearly defines its position within the window's architraves.

Techniques

To make beautiful curtains and blinds you need some essential tools and techniques at your fingertips. Read on for measuring, calculating fabric requirements, cutting and stitching, and then discover some stylish finishing techniques.

Tools and Equipment

Curtain-making is basically a highly creative and therapeutic pastime involving straightforward skills that anyone can pick up instantly. What is ideal is if you can have a room, or a corner of a room, with a table always set up so you that do not have to clear things away too often when it's time for lunch or homework or a game of Scrabble or cards. It is a huge feeling of satisfaction when those curtains are actually hanging – to think that you successfully designed, executed, sewed and hung the whole project. You know that that window treatment will be good for 20-25 years.

The basic tools and materials that you need for curtain making are few and easy to get hold of. The smaller items are featured in the photograph opposite. In addition, a trestle table is extremely useful if you have the space. This is much longer than the usual kitchen table and so makes it easier to cope with the vast lengths of fabric. Shown here (starting in the top left-hand corner and working down in columns to the bottom right-hand corner) are:

Narrow rufflette Use this for puff-ball headings (*see pages 44-47*).

Pencil pleat tape Deep 15 cm (8 in) wide. Use this for Italian-strung curtains (*see pages 34-39*) and deep smocking (*see pages 40-43*).

Pencil pleat tape Ordinary 8 cm (3¼ in) wide. Use this for the heading of all curtains that you intend to cover with a pelmet.

Piping cord (size no. 6) Use for piping details in pelmets, blinds or tiebacks, and also useful for making a swag template (*see page 82*).

Clamps A pair of metal clamps are invaluable for keeping large pieces of fabric from falling off your worksurface.

Scissors You would use the little pair as you sew various parts of your curtain, blind or pelmet. You need the big pair for cutting out all fabrics. Ensure that your fabric scissors are kept purely for cutting fabric and don't become general purpose scissors for any manner of household chores.

Small metal ruler This is brilliant for constant measuring while actually sewing the curtain. It is also incredibly useful for scraping down a fold to produce a sharp, visible line (*see page 29*).

Wooden folding ruler 2 m (6 ft) A ruler like this is an absolute must for measuring window widths and heights. This enables you to do so with such ease, speed, precision and accuracy – and you never have to climb a ladder.

String with a teaspoon To use when stuffing a ruched-band or caterpillar tieback with interlining (*see page 116*).

Lead weights To sew at every curtain corner and seam join (*see page 30*).

Brass curtain hooks Use these to hang your curtains when using pencil-pleat tapes or narrow rufflette.

Silver pin hooks Use when hanging any kind of decoratively pleated curtains off a pole or covered fascia board (*see page 75*).

White plastic runners These run along your metal rail into which you put your hooks. You can remove or add as many as you like.

Coloured embroidery skein You use this when making your smocking stitches (*see pages 42-43*).

Self-covered metal buttons These are made in various sizes, are easy to cover and look very stylish on a handmade pleat or as part of a smocking design.

Wooden doweling rods You have to insert these in Roman blinds for them to hang and work correctly (*see pages 96-99*).

Coloured thread Select the correct colour to match your fabric.

Calculator You cannot live without this in terms of working out fabric quantities, pattern repeats and handmade pleat sizes.

Bradawl This is a smashing little tool for making holes in timber when you need to insert screw-eyes when hanging Roman blinds or when attaching wall cleats or tie-back hooks.

Screw driver You would use this when attaching a brass cleat to the wall for Roman blinds, or any other piece of hardware such as pelmet boards and curtain rails.

Tieback hooks Attach these to the wall for tie-backs.

Brass S-hooks These are used horizontally to separate the cords in the pulley system of a rail. They can also be used vertically to lower the curtain where it falls onto the floor.

Metal rings Alternative to white plastic rings (*see below*).

Screw-eyes These are used to hold the cord in place when hanging a Roman or Austrian blind.

White plastic rings You need these for channelling the cord in Roman or Austrian blinds.

Cleats Small fittings to screw to the wall behind a blind around which you tie the cords.

Staple gun and staples All Velcro is attached with staples and all pelmets are hung using Velcro. A staple gun is also useful for covering the wooden batten at the top of a Roman blind (*see page 99*).

Brass acorns or curtain weights and spare rubber rings You need to attach these to the bottom of curtain cords for pulling the curtains. The rubber rings around their centres tend to perish every few years and will need replacing.

Long sharp needles These are known as 'long darners' and enable you to sew with great speed as you can make good long stitches with them. They also have large eyes so they are very easy to thread which

is particularly useful when using a six-stranded embroidery skein.

Extra long glass-headed pins Once you have used these you will never go back to short ones again!

Fusible buckram 15 cm (8 in) wide You will need this when making any of those handmade pleats like the French, dovetail or quintet pleats featured on pages 67-71. You would also need it when making a stiffened band in a pelmet or tie-back.

Lining and interlining On pages 12-13 I have already written about the wide choice of fabrics that are available for curtain and blind making and how to make your

choice. However, there are two other very important ingredients that need to be considered: lining and interlining.

Lining The best lining fabric to use is a pure cotton sateen which comes in two widths: 120 cm (48 in) and 137 cm (54 in). It is better to use the wider measure as it means you will be joining fewer widths together if you are making extra wide curtains. Coloured linings are available, but it is better to choose from the range of neutral shades as the colours can fade all too quickly, especially if your window faces south or west. There are various neutral colours and these are ivory (my favourite as the dirt shows less quickly), white, ecru and beige. If ivory isn't available, go for ecru next; beige can be terribly dark.

Interlining The invisible ingredient of curtain making, curtains made with interlining have a beautiful heavy feel to them and they hang so well, too. You can buy interlining, also known as bump, in various weights, but I choose to use medium weight for all my curtains. Anything denser, and the curtains start to become rather too heavy. The only time that I use a lightweight interlining, or 'domette', is for a tail when the fabric has to fold back on itself (*see page 86*).

In addition, interlining contributes to the insulation of a room. There is nothing like that cosy feeling when you close those lovely curtains, of a winter evening, shutting out the night. Interlined curtains obviously preserve the heat in the room so it is essential that you never put radiators under any windows where interlined curtains are going to hang. In addition, at night all the heat will sit behind the curtains and intense heat on 100 per cent cotton interlining (which may at times also pick up a little bit of damp) will cause shrinkage, slightly damaging your beautiful curtains.

Measuring Windows

Taking careful measurements for curtains, pelmets or blinds is always time well spent.
Write everything down and be prepared to measure everything twice as a double-check. Each
project in this book has detailed instructions, but read these pages for further information.

Measuring Windows for Curtains

Height

The instructions given below are for measuring the height of full length curtains which, unless there is a good reason for not having them, such as having an obstruction like a radiator in the way, are always preferable. If you are making shorter length curtains, such as those shown on page 52 in this book, measure from just below the window sill to the bottom of the pole or pelmet board.

1 Pick up your 2 m (6 ft) folding ruler, nothing else will do. You can get by using a metal tape measure or a soft tape measure, but for speed, accuracy and efficiency these are wildly inefficient.

2 Hold the ruler vertically up the side of the window, leaning it against the architrave so that the foot of the ruler with the 2 m (6 ft) end is on the floor. Make a small, light mark on the window frame with a pencil, where the top of the ruler comes to.

3 Feed the ruler on up, until you reach the top of the architrave. If this is very high up, you will have to ask a friend to stand away from the window to tell you when the ruler is level with the top of the architrave. This is where you will place the bottom of the pelmet board, assuming that you like the height of the window as it is. Note down the two measurements and add them together.

4 If you want to gain height, you merely place the pelmet board above the top of the architrave – by as much as you require. This space, above the window, is dead wall any way and can be used very efficiently

within the pelmet area by incorporating it in the overall drop of your pelmet. There are two great advantages of doing this: you raise the window height, and you can add to the finished drop of the pelmet. Length is elegance in all window treatments, so all this is of great advantage to you.

Width

The chart below will guide you in the calculations of the size of the housing space. Allow 10 per cent of the width of your window as the housing space at either side of your window and you will always be fine.

1 Hold the ruler at waist height and measure from outer edge to outer edge of the architrave.

2 Allow for housing space on either side of the window to enable the curtains to stack back, well off the window and to let in maximum light.

CURTAIN WIDTHS AND HOUSING SPACE REQUIRED FOR A WINDOW

The number of curtain widths given here is approximate and is based on material that is 137 cm (54 in) wide, and curtains that are interlined with a medium-weight interlining.

Window width (from edge of architrave to edge of architrave)	housing space (each side of window)	no. of widths in each curtain
50 cm (1 ft 8 in)	5 cm (2 in)	½
80 cm (2 ft 7 in)	1.7 cm (2¾ in)	1
1.25 m (4 ft 1 in)	10 cm (4 in)	1½
1.6 m (5 ft 3 in)	15 cm (6 in)	2
1.9 m (6 ft 3 in)	15 cm (6 in)	2
2.4 m (7 ft 11 in)	20 cm (8 in)	2½
2.8 m (9 ft 2½ in)	25 cm (10 in)	3
3.3 m (10 ft 10 in)	30 cm (12 in)	3½
3.8 m (12 ft 6 in)	30 cm (12 in)	4

Measuring Windows for Pelmets

Drop

1 Tie a handkerchief at the point on your wooden ruler where you think the finished drop of your pelmet ought to be.

2 Now ask a friend to hold up the ruler, level to where the top of your pelmet board will be. Your eye can now so easily lock onto where the finished drop of the pelmet is going to be.

3 You can then walk away from it and assess if you have made the right decision. At this point, you can take into consideration all those vital other factors involved in designing the perfect window treatment (*see pages 10-11*).

Width

1 Measure the window width, from architrave to architrave and add housing space, as outlined in the chart opposite.

2 Then add the pelmet board returns. This is now the finished width that your pelmet must be. A sample measurement is given below.

CALCULATING THE WIDTH OF A PELMET BOARD: *an example*

Window width (architrave to architrave)	1.25 m (4 ft 1 in)
Add housing space (see chart opposite): 15 cm (6 in) x 2	20 cm (8 in)
	TOTAL: 1.45 m (4 ft 9 in)

The fullness that you put into the pelmet depends on which design you have chosen and guidelines are given with each window treatment in this book. Basically, they are:

Smocked: twice the finished width

Pencil pleated, French, goblet, spaced box-pleats: two and half times the finished width

Dovetail, quintet, stand-up on Velcro, close box-pleats: three times the finished width

However, remember that on French, goblet, dovetail and quintet pleats, you must not include the returns in the 2½ or 3 x measurement. You do not put these large bulky pleats on the actual return of the pelmet board.

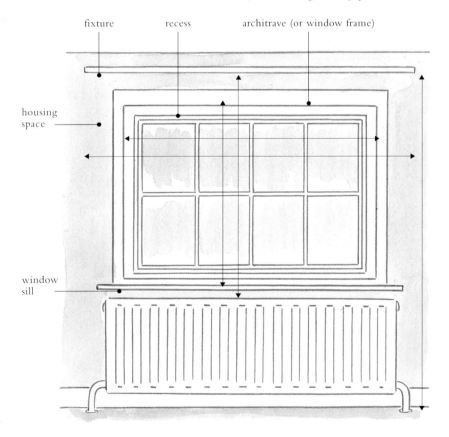

fixture recess architrave (or window frame)

housing space

window sill

Measuring Windows for Blinds

There are two positions for a Roman blind in a window. If it is recessed, take your measurements as near to the glass as possible. For the height, measure from the top of where the mounting batten will be positioned to the sill. For the width measure from one side of the recess to the other.

If the window is not recessed, you are more likely to want to hang your Roman blind over the frame. If possible, attach the mounting batten to the frame itself, but if it isn't flat enough, screw it to the wall just above the frame and take your measurements accordingly.

Calculating Quantities of Fabric

When you are making a pair of curtains, you will inevitably be handling large amounts of fabrics at a time. So calculate the quantities required very accurately to keep wastage to a minimum. The instructions given here are based on average fullness of two-and-a-half times the width. If any treatment varies, fullness details are given at the appropriate place in the book.

Curtains

Width

1 Multiply your window width by two and a half. This will give you a good fullness for your curtains and yet will not be too full.

2 Divide this figure by the width of your fabric and now you can see how many widths you will need to cut for the pair.

For example, if your window width is 1.25 m (4 ft 1 in) and your housing space is a total of 20 cm (8 in) you will have to make a total fabric width of 3.32 m (11 ft). The usual width for curtain fabric is 137 cm (54 in). So, 3.32 m divided by 137 cm (11 ft divided by 54 in) is 2½. To ensure that you have enough fabric for the seams and any extra fullness you may require for the rails overlapping at the centre, round up the widths to three; three widths of fabric are needed for a window this wide. (*See the chart on page 108 for a quick reference guide.*)

Now you will need to calculate the length of fabric that you need to make the curtains.

Length

The length of fabric needed to make a curtain will obviously vary from treatment to treatment and specific requirements are given for each design in this book. However, instructions are given here for a standard pair of pencil-pleated curtains. The principles of making allowances for pattern repeats should always be borne in mind when making your calculations.

1 To begin, subtract 2 cm (¾ in) from the under board to floor measurement. This is because the curtains hang off a rail that also hangs below the board.

2 Then add 20 cm (8 in) to the length. This will allow for you to turn up 12 cm (5 in) at the hem and 8 cm (3 in) at the top.

3 Finally, add the length of a pattern repeat to this drop. It is best to do this now to ensure that you really do have enough fabric – it is the worst thing to run short right in the middle of a curtain project.

So, if your under board to floor measurement is, say, 2.8 m (9 ft 2¼ in), subtract 2 cm (¾ in) from the measurement (2.78 m [9 ft 1½ in]), and then add 20 cm (8 in), making 2.98 m (9 ft 9½ in). Then add the size of the pattern repeat – say, 40 cm (15½ in) - making a total of 3.4 m (11 ft 2 in).

4 For the grand total, multiply 3.4 m (11 ft 2 in) by the number of widths of fabric (3), leaving you with 10.2 m (33 ft 6 in or 11¼ yds) – round this up to 10.5 m – (11½ yd) of fabric to buy.

Pelmets

Allow at least a 7 cm (2¾ in) hem at the lower edge. The turning at the top depends on what style you have chosen, as does the fullness and specific instructions are given with each different style of pelmet in the book.

Fixing Pelmet Boards and Rails

The pelmet board and rail should really be fixed above the window before you measure up for your curtains. However, this is not always possible and when it comes to hanging your curtains you may find them too long or short. There are ways round this described on page 124.

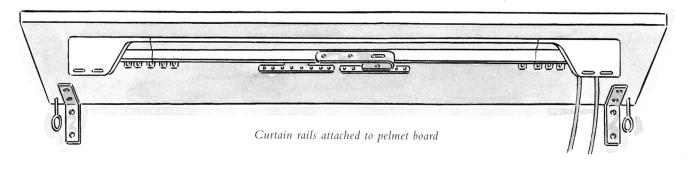

Curtain rails attached to pelmet board

Pelmet boards

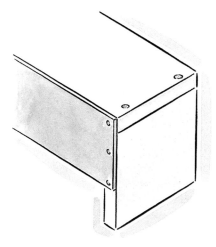

ABOVE *Pelmet board with plywood fascia and timber return*

The wood for a pelmet board should be 17 cm (7 in) deep and 2 cm (¾ in) thick. Its length will be determined by the size of your window treatment, including the housing space, and should be cut most precisely or you will find your curtains and pelmets don't fit especially well when hung. Use either timber or blockboard.

If you are hanging a pelmet that has a fusible buckram band at its top (*for example, see page 65*), you will need a plywood fascia along the front of the board and vertical timber returns made from the same type of wood as the pelmet board. Each return should measure 17 cm (7 in) square. Screw the returns into the ends and fix the plywood to the front of the pelmet board.

Use a pair of strong angle brackets to attach the pelmet board to the wall. If the width is over 1.3 m (4 ft 3 in) put a bracket in the centre as well. There is no need to paint pelmet boards as all the visible parts will be covered with the pelmet itself.

Rails

Use only strong metal rails with an in-built pulley system and top fix them straight onto the pelmet board, setting it approximately 8 cm (3¼ in) from the front of the board. Make sure that the rail stops well clear of the end so that the curtains are able to turn a right angled corner and travel in to the wall to keep out any drafts. To prevent the edge of the curtains from moving away from the wall when pulled close, suspend the last hook on a large 4 cm (1¾ in) long brass screw-eye positioned outside the angled bracket.

Measuring and Cutting Material

*Before measuring, cutting or joining any material, it is essential to check that the grain
of the material is straight along the starting edge. To do this, it is easiest
to use the square angles of your cutting table, as explained below. Once the material
is straight and even, you can start measuring out, cutting and joining widths.
At every stage, make use of table clamps which will hold the material in place and
make these jobs infinitely easier.*

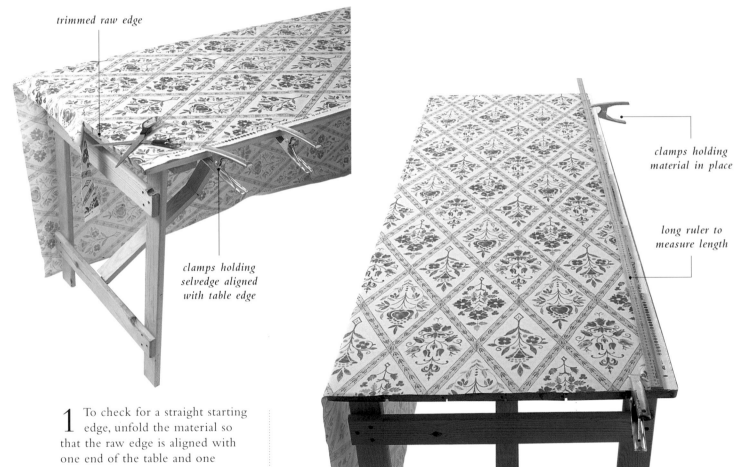

trimmed raw edge

clamps holding
selvedge aligned
with table edge

clamps holding
material in place

long ruler to
measure length

1 To check for a straight starting
edge, unfold the material so
that the raw edge is aligned with
one end of the table and one
selvedge aligned with the long edge
of the table. Clamp the material to
the table to hold it in place. Then,
running the scissors along the end
of the table, trim the edge to
straighten it.

2 First, check your calculations and measurements to make sure that they
are correct, and that you have enough fabric. With the starting edge still
level with one end of the table, unroll the material the whole length of the
table and clamp it in place, keeping one selvedge aligned with the long edge.
Using the 2 m (6 ft) folding ruler, measure down along the selvedge as far as
the table will allow and mark the selvedge. Then unclamp and unroll more
material, moving it onto the table. Again, measure along the selvedge until the
total cutting length is reached, and mark the selvedge.

Unclamp, move back to the beginning of the material and measure down
the other selvedge in the same way.

3 In order to mark the cutting line, place the folding ruler across the table and join up the two final marks on the selvedges. Draw a line across the material, running the pen along the ruler. Cut along the line using straight-edged scissors.

4 To cut the remaining widths of material, unroll another quantity and clamp it to the table in the same way as the first width. Take the first width, already cut, and match its pattern by lining it up temporarily with the uncut material. Make a mark on the selvedge to indicate where the next length of fabric will begin. Measure the distance from the mark just made to the top of the material, so that you can now mark the opposite selvedge the same distance from the top. This removes any excess of pattern repeat, so that the pattern will match at the seams. You are now ready to cut the second width. Repeat the same process as cutting the first width.

ruler showing cutting line

Joining Widths and Pattern Matching

Selvedges

Selvedges are rarely cut off on any material. On some fabrics, however, writing along the selvedge may be rather prominent. It is important that the writing does not show through, so it has to be cut off. This particularly applies to curtains, where light shines through. The selvedge may also cause a problem if it is rather tight, which is sometimes the case with linen. In this case, it is sufficient to snip the selvedge intermittently, in order to ease it.

selvedge turned under and pattern matched

1 Clamp the first width of material to the table, right side up, with the selvedge running along the long edge of the table and the top of the material at one end (*see step 1, opposite*).

Take the second width and line up its selvedge (also right side up) with the first width on the table so that the pattern matches. Turn under the selvedge of the second width and pin it to the clamped width, matching the pattern carefully. Insert the pins parallel to the turned-under selvedge and place them about 20 cm (8 in) apart.

Stitches

Use a long sharp needle at all times and always make a strong knot at the end of your thread before you start sewing. Always finish off your thread securely when you finish a row of stitching by making several small over-stitches.

Interlocking

This stitch is used for locking either the interlining to the lining, or the main fabric to the interlining. Always stop these stitches 20 cm (8 in) from the top and the bottom of the curtain.

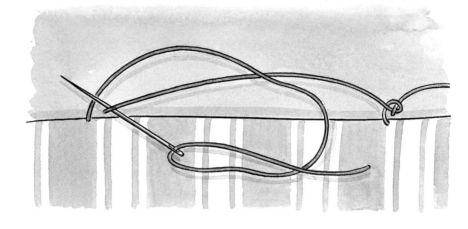

1 With the curtain fabric folded back on itself, start the row of interlocking stitches by passing the needle through a few grains of the fabric at this fold and then stab through the interlining underneath it and come up again, having made one running stitch.

2 To make the next stitch, repeat the same process 13 cm (5 in) further along the fabric. But there is one difference: after you come up from the interlining, take your needle so that it loops through the thread that is already in place, coming from the previous stitch.

Pyramid Stitch

Pyramid stitch is used on curtains when securing the raw edge of the main fabric, once turned over onto the interlining. Stop all stitches 20 cm (8 in) from both the top and bottom of the curtain.

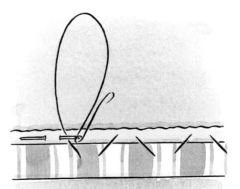

1 Come up from behind the top fabric, approximately 1 cm (½ in) from its raw edge.

2 Take the needle through the interlining at a diagonal from where you have just come out, thus forming the first side of the pyramid. You come out 1 cm (½ in) from where you went into the interlining.

3 Now stitch back onto the main fabric, again approximately 1 cm (½ in) from its raw edge.

Slip Stitch

This stitch is used for sewing down the edge of the lining of curtains, the hems and many other places where an invisible method of closing is necessary.

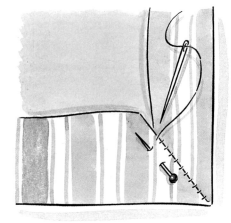

1 Come from under the fold with your needle, leaving the knot under the fold and hidden. Come out right at the edge of the fold.

2 Now go back into the other fabric (which is under the fold) at exactly the place where you have just come out. Having gone back in here, now run your needle along as far as it will go, within the fold of the under fabric, and come out on the upper fold again. This leads to an invisible stitch.

Stab Stitch

Stab stitch is used when securing handmade pleats on pelmets, curtains or swags and tails.

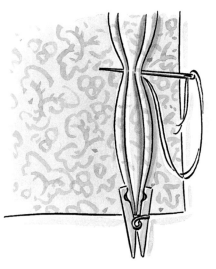

1 Using matching doubled thread, pass the needle backwards and forwards through your pleat. Push the needle straight through all the layers of fabric and repeat four times to make a strong and secure closure. You are below the fusible buckram here. With each stitch you make, you step nearer the fold of the pleats.

Tiebacks and Heading Details

These are the finishing touch on many a well-made pair of curtains. A plaited tieback is featured on page 49, and a caterpiller tieback on page 45. To turn tubes like those below, an alternative method is to stitch a piece of string within the tube at the short end and then pull it to turn it through.

Plaited

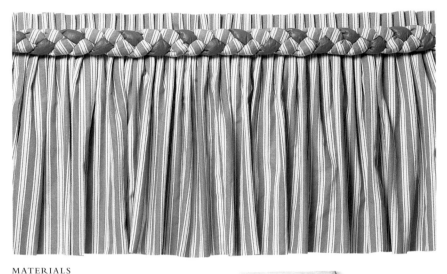

Preparation

CUT THREE PIECES OF FABRIC; two in the main fabric and one in a contrast. Make each one 9 cm (3½ in) wide, including 3 cm (1¼ in) seam allowances, and long enough to plait to the required length. Fold each piece of fabric in half lengthways and with right sides facing. Machine across one end and down the long side. Trim the seams and turn right sides out pushing the tube over a screw driver or wooden spoon pushed against the seamed end. Cut off the seamed end. Cut three pieces of interlining 13 cm (5 in) wide and to the same length as the fabric tubes.

MATERIALS

main fabric   interlining
contrast fabric   tieback rings

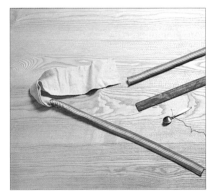

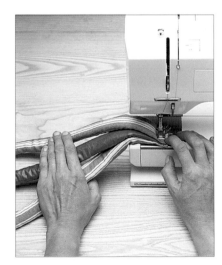

1 To fill each tube, pull interlining through using a piece of string attached to one end of the interlining and the other tied onto a spoon. When the interlining appears at the other end of the tube, stop pulling and remove the string. Trim the interlining at each end of the tube so that it is 2 cm (¾ in) shorter than the face fabric.

2 Stitch together the three tubes, one on top of the other with the contrast fabric in the centre. Run back and forth across the tubes several times to ensure they are firmly fixed.

3 Clamp the tubes onto the edge of your worksurface and plait to the required length. Once finished, machine across the ends as in step 2.

4 Cut a piece of binding for each end measuring 12 x 7 cm (4½ x 3 in). Press in half widthways with right sides facing and machine around two sides taking a 1 cm (½ in) seam allowance. Turn right sides out and poke out the corners.

5 Feed the 'shoes' onto each end of the tieback, and pin and slipstitch into place turning under the seam allowance as you work. If you are making a plait for a pelmet, don't worry about making shoes for each end. Instead, turn back the end seam and stab stitch into place.

6 Attach a brass ring to the centre back at each end of the tieback.

Caterpillar

Preparation

Make a fabric tube as for the plait (four times the caterpillar's finished length) and press with the seam centred to the back. Stuff with interlining, as for the plait, but cut the interlining to 17 cm (6½ in) wide. Machine stitch across the end to thoroughly secure the interlining.

MATERIALS *main fabric*
interlining

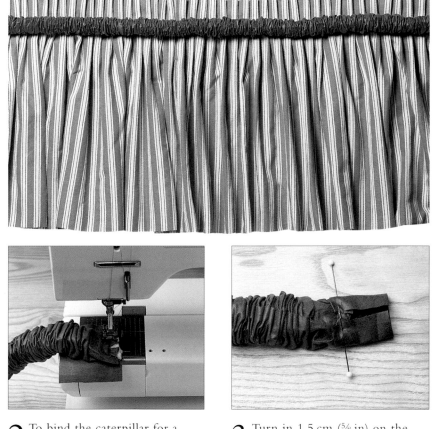

1 Clamp the fabric to the edge of a table and ruche up the fabric on the interlining. When you have achieved the correct length, machine across the other end, as before.

2 To bind the caterpillar for a tieback, cut a piece of fabric 6 cm (2¼ in) wide and long enough to wrap over the end of the tube (approximately 5 cm [2 in]). Lay the binding on the end with right sides facing and raw edges aligned, and centred so that 1.5 cm (⅝ in) is left on each side. Stitch in place taking a 1.5 cm (⅝ in) seam allowance.

3 Turn in 1.5 cm (⅝ in) on the remaining raw edges, and fold the binding in half over the end of the tieback. Hand sew in place. Bind the other end in the same way.

Choux Rosette

A CHOUX ROSETTE is a very decorative detail and can be used successfully in place of a Maltese Cross at the top of Italian-strung curtains (see page 35) or, indeed, any other fixed heading. A rosette is all too easily squashed, so keep it in a safe place (I would keep mine in a box) before attaching to your curtain heading. If you should want to make a larger choux than the one featured below, cut the centre circle to a 12 cm (4½ in) diameter, make the square of fabric 35-38 cm (14-15 in) square and use interlining. Make 15 pleats in the fabric for step 4, opposite.

MATERIALS

main fabric
fusible buckram
interlining

1 Cut out a 10 cm (4 in) diameter circle of fusible buckram. Repeat for two circles of interlining and iron into place on each side of the buckram. Draw a cross on one side of the circle. Then cut out a 30 cm (12 in) square of fabric.

2 Hand-stitch the edge of one quarter of the fabric on to one quarter of the circle, taking small pleats. Keep them as even as possible, but if you find you are running out of fabric right at the end of the circle, don't worry, the end result will still look good. As you reach each corner, neatly include it with a pleat.

3 When all four sides are stitched, pull out the fabric over the sides.

4 On the front of the choux, arrange the folds in the fabric using the fingers of one hand to position them. Make about nine pleats.

5 Stab stitch at the base of each pleat to keep it in place.

6 On the back, pin a circle of fabric in place, folding under a 1.5 cm (⅝ in) seam allowance as you work. Slip stitch in place.

Frills, Piping and Tufts

Here are three finishing touches (frills, below; piping, opposite; and tufts, overleaf)
that will give any window treatment a truly professional finish.
When adding any decorative details like this, take your time: the end results will be worth it.

Frills

A gathered frill (2½ x fullness)

For a 6 cm (2¼ in) wide frill, cut strips of fabric 14 cm (5½ in) wide. Cut enough strips to be 2½ times the finished length of your frill. Join strips as necessary (there is no need to worry about pattern matching). Looking at the right side of the fabric, fold in 2 cm (1¾ in) and scrape with a sharp metal ruler. Then fold the strip in half, lengthways, with wrong sides together. Machine stitch along the length, taking a 1 cm (½ in) seam allowance, press.

MATERIALS   *main fabric*
contrast fabric
(optional)

A pleated frill (3 x fullness)

1 To gather the fabric, make the gathers as you stitch. Pinch small 1 cm (½ in) pleats and machine along the seam allowance. If you are using a chintz, lick your fingers lightly to prevent the fabric from slipping. Don't press. To make bigger pleats, work in exactly the same way, but make 2 cm (¾ in) pleats instead and press the strip once you have finished.

Variation: pleated frill with contrast top and bottom

Cut the contrast strip to 9 cm (3½ in) wide and the main strip to 7 cm (2¾ in) wide. Stitch together with right sides facing, trim the seams and then turn through as described on page 116. Press the strip with the front fabric centred between the contrast borders at top and bottom. Work with care on the ironing board and using your small metal ruler.

Piping

This is an unusual but very fast way of cutting fabric strips on the bias. Once you have got used to pinning together the two triangles of fabric you will never want to return to the more conventional method.

MATERIALS

main fabric

piping cord

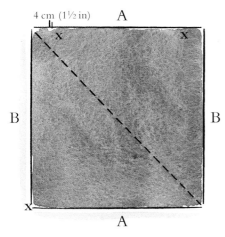

1 Cut a square of fabric, cut in half diagonally and mark with letters as on the diagram.

2 Join A to A with right sides facing and carefully matching the Xs. Machine stitch the side together taking a 1.5 cm (⅝ in) seam allowance.

3 Join B to B, matching the corner with the A-A seam. Machine stitch, again taking a 1.5 cm (⅝ in) seam allowance. Press seams open.

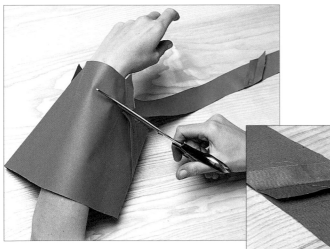

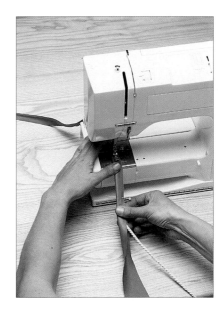

4 Still with the wrong side on the outside, slip the circle of fabric over your non-cutting hand's wrist and cut a 4 cm (1½ in) wide strip starting at the marking. Cut continuously using a ruler every now and then to ensure consistency of the width. Do not worry when you get the occasional bulging strip at the seams. This is inevitable and can be rectified by a quick neaten with the scissors.

5 Set in the piping folding the strip around the piping cord with wrong sides together and raw edges aligned. Stitch with a 1.5 cm (⅝ in) seam allowance.

Tufts

Although each tuft is small, when you stitch them onto each pleat of a pleated pelmet, say, their combined effect is very striking (*see page 72*).

1 Wrap the wool around your index and middle fingers twenty times (if you are using thicker wool, wrap it ten times).

2 Remove the loops from your fingers pinching them tightly in the centre. Wrap the wool around the centre five times. Still holding the tuft tightly with one hand, cut off the wool from the ball and thread a large-eyed bobbin with the excess and pass it through the centre of the tuft several times to secure it. Then stitch it very neatly to the curtain heading.

Once you have made a few tufts you will know how much wool you need for each one. Then you can cut off the appropriate lengths before winding around your fingers and thread the needle at the far end. This will make step 2 far more straightforward.

Hanging, Dressing and Altering Lengths

Now that all the hard work is over, you reach the moment of truth: will the treatment fit?
Of course, if you have measured accurately and then sewn precisely there is no reason why they shouldn't
look just as you had imagined them. There are a few things you can do to help them look as good
as possible and this starts with the hanging. Do this as soon as possible after you have made the curtains
so that they don't crease. If you can't manage this within a day or so of making them, don't fold
them up but leave them draped carefully over the back of a chair or the stair rail.

Hanging

1 Count the number of runners (including the overlap arm and screw-eyes at the returns of the board) on your rail and ensure that the number of hooks on the top of the curtain correspond.

2 Climb a pair of step ladders (with someone else in the house who vaguely knows what you are doing) with one of the curtains over your shoulder.

3 Feed the hooks into the runners starting at the far end of the rail (do not start in the centre as it puts a strain on the overlap arm). At the far end, the first two hooks go through a screw eye and part of the rail joint. If you have a seam join with half a width of fabric, the whole width always goes nearest to the centre.

4 Check that the curtains close and open correctly with sufficient overlap at the centre before finally securing the strings that pull up the heading tape. The strings always pull up at the outside edges and they should be knotted carefully and the strings hidden from view.

Dressing

Dressing your curtains is the finishing touch as this ensures that the pleats hang regularly and neatly. The fabric needs some encouragement to do this, but once dressed, there will be no need to do it again and it is worth spending time at this stage for the most professional finished result.

1 At chest level, pleat the curtains evenly between your hands, keeping the pleats in place by pressing them against your chest as you go. Once you have reached the other end of the curtain, tie string (or a strip of remnant fabric) around it. Tie the string firmly, yet you do not want to cause creasing. Repeat this process in about five places, moving from the top to the bottom of the curtain.

2 Clap your hands hard together, with the curtain in-between. This will encourage the pleats to stay in place. Then leave them tied up for five days. I know this is agony since you are dying to pull them but, honestly, it is worth it for the long-term look of the curtains.

Dressing a curtain. By carefully pleating the curtains and then tying them to encourage the pleats to stay in place you will ensure your curtains look as good as possible.

Altering lengths

Just occasionally you may find that your curtains are a fraction too long or too short. The only time when you can do anything about this, however, is if you have pencil-pleated curtains whose heading is covered by a pelmet.

If they are too short, you have three alternative methods for rectifying the problem:

1 Move the hooks into the bottom two strands of the pencil pleat tape (your hooks should already have been in the top hook position).

2 Fix a wooden spacer between the rail and the pelmet board at each end. A spacer is a 8 mm (¼ in) thick wooden disc with a diameter of 2 cm (¾ in) and a hole in the middle through which you can thread a screw. These will make the rail a fraction lower.

3 Feed S-hooks onto the runners of the rail by opening each one with a pair of pliers, hanging it and then closing it again. Now you can hang the curtains off each S-hook. S-hooks come in various sizes ranging from 2 cm (¾ in) to 5 cm (2 in) in length, so buy those that are appropriate for your problem.

For curtains that are too long, you have two ways to tackle the problem:

1 Move the hooks to the bottom position of the pencil pleat tape, and up go the curtains.

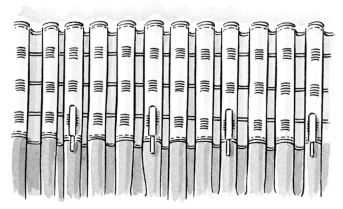

2 Fix a wooden spacer between the angle bracket and the pelmet board at each end. These will make the whole board will go up, taking the curtains with it.

RIGHT *Here the curtains are puddling fashionably on the floor, but if you prefer them shorter there are ways to rectify the problem (see above).*

Suppliers

UK

Lady Caroline Wrey
60 The Chase
London SW3 0NH
Telephone: 0171 622 6625
(*Table clamps, folding rulers, small metal rulers, long pins and long needles*)

Abbey Quilters
Selina's Lane
Dagenham
Essex
RM8 1ES
Telephone: 0181 592 2233
(*Quilters*)

Karen Ashley
3 Algores Way
Weasenham Lane
Wisbech
Cambs PE13 2TQ
Telephone: 01945 589595
(*Quilters*)

Ciment Pleating
39b Church Hill Road
Church Hill
Walthamstow
London E17 9RX
Telephone: 0181 520 0415
(*Permanent pleaters*)

Classic Quilters
217 Dawes Road
London SW6 7QZ
Telephone: 0171 385 1872
(*Quilters*)

Elite (Mr Bushky)
27 Churton Street
London SW1
Telephone: 0171 834 0753
(*Cleaners*)

Hallis and Hudson Group Ltd
Bushell Street
Preston
Lancashire PR1 2SP
Telephone: 01772 202202
Fax: 01772 889889
(*Plain coloured chintzes*)

Hesse and Co
Waring and Gillow Estate
Western Avenue
London W3 0TA
Telephone: 0181 992 2212
Fax: 0181 752 0012
(*Interlinings and linings*)

Holbein
Wrafton Works
Rear of 45 Evelyn Road
London SW19 8NT
Telephone: 0181 542 2422
Fax: 0181 542 5222
(*Highly decorative poles*)

Hunter and Hyland Ltd
201-201 Kingston Road
Leatherhead
Surrey KT22 7PB
Telephone: 01372 378511
Fax: 01372 370038
(*Interlinings, linings and curtain hanging materials*)

John Lewis Partnership
(*all branches*)
278-306 Oxford Street
London W1A 1EX
Telephone: 0171 629 7711
Fax: 0171 629 0849
(*Sewing equipment, fabrics, sheeting and curtain hanging accessories*)

Marvic Textiles Ltd
Unit 1
Westpoint Trading Estate
Alliance Road
Acton
London W3 0RA
Telephone: 0181 993 0191
Fax: 0181 993 1484
(*Fabrics*)

Porter Nicholson
Portland House
Norlington Road
London EC10 6JX
Telephone: 0181 539 6106
Fax: 0181 558 9200
(*Interlinings and linings*)

Marion Petschi
32 Drewstead Road
London SW16 1AB
Telephone: 0181 769 4606
(*Curtain maker*)

GJ Turner and Co
Fitzroy House
Abbot Street
London E8 3DP
Telephone: 0171 254 8187
Fax: 0171 254 8471
(*Trimmings*)

Brian Wright Esq
PO Box 2
24 Ventura Road
Falmouth
Cornwall TR11 3XB
(*Covered buttons*)

FRANCE

Linum
ZI La Grande Marine
84800 Isle-sur-la-Sorgue
France
Telephone: 90 38 37 38
Fax: 90 38 21 53
(*Fabrics*)

USA

ArtMark Fabric
480 Lancaster Pike
Frazer
PA 19355
Telephone: 1 800 523 0362
(*Plain coloured chintzes*)

Calico Corners
(*national chain*)
745 Lancaster Pike
Strafford
Wayne
PA 19087
Telephone: 215 688 1505
(*Fabric and sewing equipment*)

Cleantex Process Co Inc
2335 12th Avenue
New York, NY
Telephone: 212 283 1200
(*Cleaners*)

DownRight Ltd
6101 16th Avenue
Brooklyn
NY 11204
Telephone: 718 232 2206
(*Cleaners*)

Gige Interiors Ltd
170 S. Main Street
Yardley
PA 19067
Telephone: 215 493 8052
(*Interlinings, linings, plain coloured chintzes and curtain hanging materials*)

Graber Products Division
Springs Window Fashions
Middleton
WI 53562
Telephone: 1 800 356 9102
(*Curtain hanging materials*)

Greentext Upholstery Supplies
Telephone: 212 206 8585
(*Table clamps and folding rulers*)

HKH Design
24 Middlefield Drive
San Francisco
CA 94132
Telephone: 415 564 2383
(*Curtain hanging materials*)

Kirsch Co
PO Box 370
Sturges
MI 49091
Telephone: 1 800 528 1407
(*Curtain hanging materials*)

M&J Trimmings
1008 Sixth Avenue
New York
NY 10018
Telephone: 212 391 9072
(*Trimmings*)

George Matuk
37 West 26th Street
New York
NY 10010
Telephone: 212 683 9242
(*Sheeting*)

Norbar Fabrics
1101 Lakeland Avenue
PO Box 528
Bohemia
NY 11716
Telephone: 1 800 645 8501
(*Plain coloured chintzes*)

SF Pleating
61 Greenpoint Avenue
Brooklyn
NY 11222
Telephone: 718 383 7950
(*Permanent pleaters*)

SF Pleating
425 Second Street
San Francisco
CA 94107
Telephone: 415 982 3003
(*Permanent pleaters*)

Author's acknowledgments

I would like to thank:

Marion Petschi, my curtain maker, for all the highly skilled and
conscientious efforts in producing the finished window treatment on time for all the
photoshoots, and for all her boundless enthusiasm for the projects.

George, my husband, for his huge support and devotion
over the production of another book.

My editor, Cindy Richards, for suggesting Collins & Brown as the publisher
for this book and for her unlimited enthusiasm and efforts
in producing the most inspiring and professional team to work with me.

Emma Callery for extremely patient and meticulous editing
and her sensitive attention to detail.

Janet James for her careful consideration of every detail of
every page resulting in a superb book design.

Kate Haxell for all her support throughout the project.

Muna Reyal for her care over the picture research.

Sam Lloyd for his brilliant step-by-step photography throughout the book.

Lucinda Symons for her utterly beautiful and artistic finished style shots.

Jacky Boase for her sensational styling in the photography – a seriously magical touch.

Sonia Pugh for her extremely energetic work relating to the publicity for the book.

The John Lewis Partnership and especially David Jones and
Evelyn Strouts for giving us so much wonderful fabric and curtain accessories
to use for all the window treatments.

Peter Afia at Marvic Textiles for giving us many metres of beautiful material.

**The publisher and author would like to thank
the following suppliers for their fabrics:**

Front cover Marvic Textiles, Misa Moiré stripe 4331/23; p24 John Lewis Partnership,
blue/white stripe; p34 Marvic Textiles, Misa Moiré stripe 'check' scarlet 6795/18;
p41 John Lewis Partnership, 'Lilac'; p44 John Lewis Partnership, 'Berkley Gold';
p48 John Lewis Partnership, 'Jungle Walk'; p52 John Lewis Partnership, 'Stowe' red
654/54730; p56 John Lewis Partnership, voile with starfish, shells and seahorses;
p64 Marvic Textiles, 'Medalion' Henrietta Spencer Churchill; p73 John Lewis
Partnership; p76 Linum, 'Mikado' harlequin; p81 Marvic Textiles, Misa Moiré stripe;
p94 John Lewis Partnership, 'Country Cottage'; p100 Linum, 'Provence'.

Index

*Page numbers in **bold** indicate photographs*

Acknowledgements

All styled photographs have been taken specially for this book by Lucinda Symons. The step-by-step photography was taken by Sampson Lloyd. All the photography on pages 64-71 is by Clive Streeter. The following appear by kind permission:

Abode UK: 25 bottom, 93 bottom. **Arcaid**: 24 bottom. **Camera Press**: London 63 right. **Robert Harding Syndication**: 91 top, Simon Brown Country Homes & Interiors 92 left, Jan Baldwin Country Homes & Interiors 60, Polly Wreford Country Homes & Interiors 20 top, 93 top, Polly Wreford Homes and Gardens 61 top right, James Merrell Homes & Gardens 61 top left, Christopher Drake Homes & Gardens 24 top right, 62 bottom left, 90 top, Tom Leighton Homes & Gardens 90 bottom, Debi Treloar Homes & Gardens 92 right, Pia Tryde Woman & Home 62 bottom right. **Houses & Interiors**: Simon Butcher 63 left. **Interior Archive**: James Mortimer 22, Fritz von der Schulenburg 24 top left, 25 top, 61 bottom, C. Simon Sykes 91 bottom, Henry Wilson 21, 23 top right, 23 bottom right. **Elizabeth Whiting Associates**: 20 bottom, 62 top.